Oh No! It's Local Rock and Roll

...but I like it!

Oh No! It's Local Rock and Roll

...but I like it!

A FOND LOOK BACK AT THE ROOTS OF ROCK AND ROLL IN MID DEVON 1954–1979

Barry Sowden

HALSGROVE

First published in Great Britain in 2002

British Library Cataloguing-in-Publication Data
A CIP record for this title is available from the British Library

ISBN 1 84114 224 7

HALSGROVE

Halsgrove House
Lower Moor Way
Tiverton, Devon EX16 6SS
Tel: 01884 243242
Fax: 01884 243325
email: sales@halsgrove.com
website: www.halsgrove.com

Printed and bound in Great Britain by Bookcraft (Bath) Ltd, Midsomer Norton

Contents

Dedication   6

Foreword   7

Acknowledgements and Special Thanks   8

Preface   9

Introduction   11

A Tribute to Bill Greenhalgh   17

THE GROUPS – PART ONE   **19**

The Bluebirds   20

The Chekkers   23

The Strollers   27

The Cyclones   33

The Stringbeats   36

The Tuxedos   41

The Echoes   43

The Falcons   47

The Starfires   51

Photograph Gallery   56

THE GROUPS – PART TWO   **61**

The Avengers   62

The Dominoes   67

The Shakey Notes and Blue Sunset   72

Nashville Skyline   75

The Hotspots   79

Something Different   84

Touch of Amber   86

The Ginger Walker Band   88

The New Bluebirds and Barracuda   91

A Band of Absent Friends   95

DEDICATION

'Mum' (or Dad, depending on which parent can be more easily manipulated),
'Can I have a guitar/drum kit/keyboard/saxophone/microphone/amplifier
(delete as necessary), for Christmas please? – I want to join a rock group!'

With Sex, Drugs, and Rock and Roll at the very top of their 'things to worry about list',
these are the words most likely to strike fear into the heart of any parent
– yet they still bought our first one!

This book is dedicated to all our Mums and Dads, with love and thanks.

Foreword

ABOUT THE AUTHOR

Born in 1948 Barry Sowden was educated at the Tiverton Grammar School. A multi-instrumentalist, he was taught to read music at an early age by his Uncle Bill, subsequently playing trombone in the local Salvation Army and Tiverton Town bands.

The author

Self-taught guitarist and keyboard player, he was a founding member of two very popular rock bands, The Avengers and Nashville Skyline, forging a musical, and almost brotherly, link with Ray Pope that was to last for over thirty years.

Following in his father's and grandfather's footsteps, Barry joined the Devon Fire Brigade in 1966 as a retained fireman at Station 44 Tiverton, serving with the unit until 1981. This practical experience was to stand him in good stead when his employer, Twose of Tiverton Ltd, part of the Lowman Engineering Group, appointed him to the post of Fire and Safety Officer. In addition Barry was editor of the company magazine.

Now aged fifty-four, Barry is married to a very tolerant Mary (he is currently learning to play the bagpipes). The couple live in Tiverton, have two children and five grandchildren.

Possessing a wealth of musical knowledge and the ability to communicate, Barry has taught many young people to play the guitar in the hope that they will derive, and give to others, as much pleasure from their music as he has.

Ginger Walker
March 2002

Acknowledgements

Reg Bagwell, Vince Beer, Cyril Blackford, Martin and Margaret Blythe, Patrick Brewer, Margaret Boax, John Bryant, Geoff Bulley, Terry Cottrell, Geoff Crozier, Paul Curgenven, Ian and Karen Daniels, Alan Ferris, Lee Flaws, Pam Ford, Brian Gibbs, Alison Goffin, Keith Gowan, Richard Gray, Una and Jane Greenhalgh, Peter Hammacott, Leonard 'Curly' Harder, Fred and Bev Harris, Rob Hayball, Mike Herniman, Ray Hill, Bernard and Carol Holland, Douglas 'Kaye' Holland, Jeff Horrell, Stuart Howe, Martin and Paul Irwin, Graham and Bridget Isaac, Bob Jarvis, Carol Jones, Richard King, Brian Knowles, Janet Le-Tocq, Phil Main, Paul Midgeley, Rod Milne, Mary Mitchell, Brian Nott, Gerald and Gill Orchard, Doug Parish, John and Judy Phripp, Tony and Shirley Rawle, Colin and Mo Roberts, Peter Slater, Darren and Lisa Sowden, Derek Sowden, Ian and Heather Sowden, Ray Sowden, Dave Walker, Colin and Stella Webber, Brian Westbrook, Peter and Edna White, Gordon Vearncombe.

SPECIAL THANKS

I am indebted to David 'Dan'l' Wood, his wife Bernice, and their son Martin – without whose help this book would still be in its infancy.

My sincere thanks are also extended to John Dray for his boundless enthusiasm – and to Ginger Walker for his professional and organisational skills.

And finally, to my wife Mary – thanks for everything.

Preface

Music in all its various forms has something for everyone, whether it be rock and roll, country, folk or classical. It has the power to uplift the soul and to move us deeply – many of us will have our own 'special song' – I know I have.

John Dray

For those of us who learn to play a musical instrument, or sing, being a member of a band brings an extra dimension to our lives. The trials and tribulations of day-to-day life are quickly forgotten when we pick up our chosen instrument and make music.

Being part of a band generates self-esteem, and creates enduring friendships – despite the odd 'artistic differences' which arise from time to time!

And so to Barry's book:

Throughout the late 1950s, the 60s and early 70s, musicians and audiences had such wonderful times that it was fitting that someone record the people, places, and events that comprise this book. Many have talked about it, but only Barry with his own memories and great love of music has made it happen.

Over the last seven months he has driven hundreds of miles in researching this book; talking to musicians, their families and friends and collecting hundreds of old photographs – often rescued from attics, farm buildings, and so on. This mammoth undertaking has been made slightly easier by the provision of many 'forgotten' photographs taken by Martin 'Stan' Blythe – then a photographer within his father's business, Gainsborough of Tiverton. Now a professional film and lighting cameraman, Martin was always an avid follower of local groups, and a musician himself.

I believe that for Barry, it has been a labour of love, and that his life has been enriched. It has however done much more: so many musicians and friends have been reunited, telephone numbers have been exchanged in profusion, lengthy phone calls (and big bills!) have ensued, reunion parties have taken place and promises to re-form bands have been made.

On behalf of everyone mentioned in this book: thank you Barry for your enthusiasm and effort in producing a work that will be treasured by all those who read it – including the families of those fondly remembered musicians sadly no longer with us.

Keep on rockin'.

John Dray
Guitarist, June 2002

Barry Sowden

Introduction

Modern technology has made it relatively easy for solo artistes, duos and bands to create their own studio sound. Fully orchestrated backing tracks, sampling facilities, and drum machines are now in regular use by both professional, and semi-professional performers.

This was definitely not the case during the period encompassed by this book. In 1954, a gentleman by the name of Lonnie Donegan entered the Decca studios to make a record, different in its entirety from anything heard previously. The record was entitled 'Rock Island Line', and was almost certainly the first commercial example of skiffle, the latest craze to invade Britain from America.

The basic simplicity of skiffle, allowed it to be played by those fortunate enough to own a guitar or banjo, using the absolute minimum number of chords, and permitted the less fortunate to join in by utilising washboards, inverted tea-chests, broom handles and string. Lacking any substantial volume, these 'instruments' were the ideal accompaniment for a singer, or singers, who had neither microphone nor amplifier.

Tiverton had its share of skiffle groups, The Duffels, The Rangers and The Domino Kids to name but three, and many of the men featured in the pages that follow began their musical career by playing this type of music.

Just one year after Donegan's hit, in 1955, American Bill Haley and his Comets, stormed into the British Hit Parade (the Charts), with a song called 'Rock Around the Clock'. Comparing skiffle with rock and roll, was akin to comparing an archbishop to Jack the Ripper. Although occasionally played at a lively pace, skiffle was invariably melodious and kind to the ear. Rock and roll was loud, always played at a frantic pace, loved by teenagers, and despised by the majority of parents everywhere.

Local businessman Douglas 'Kaye' Holland the proprietor of a snack bar in West Exe North, Tiverton, was asked by his younger clientele to acquire a jukebox for the café. Realising the need for a music licence, Kaye duly attended the local magistrates court and was informed by the chairman of the bench, Sir John Heathcoat-Amory, that the request would be granted on the express condition that music only be played between the hours of 9am and 9pm. Sir John stressed that failure to comply with this ruling would lead to the licence being revoked, and that representatives of the Town Council would make periodic visits to the premises.

Douglas 'Kaye' Holland.

Kaye supervised installation of the Bel-Ami jukebox, complete with its library of 100 records. He ensured that a small number of records were of the easy-listening variety by artists such as Frank Sinatra, Nat King Cole and Mantovani. These were to be played during a visit by council officials. On completion of such visits, a 'mole', strategically positioned outside the Labour Exchange on West Exe corner, would nonchalantly observe the party reach the centre of the bridge over the River Exe, give the all-clear signal to Kaye, and the snack bar would again reverberate to the sounds of Little Richard and Jerry Lee Lewis.

The mutual trust that developed between Kaye and his adolescent charges was remarkable. He became a father-figure, advisor and, in one or two cases, unofficial probation officer, and the teenagers responded with respect and good behaviour, until that is, the day of the 'Teddy Boys' Picnic'.

Seeking to give the youngsters something in return for their patronage, Kaye hired a bus and announced that he would accompany 40 boys and girls on a day-trip to Paignton and Torquay. The outing was immediately christened the Teddy Boys' Picnic. On 15 February 1958, together with the Duffels skiffle group, Kaye and his entourage set off for the coast where they spent a most enjoyable day.

The police officer who spoke to Kaye the next morning said that he was in no doubt as to who was responsible for the wrecked toilet block on the outskirts of Torquay, or the missing plants from both Paignton and Torquay seafronts, but that he had only circumstantial evidence. He did, however, suggest that an outing of this type not take place again. Kaye conducted his own investigation to find the alleged culprits, but was met with, in his words, 'the finest set of alibis I've ever heard'.

The Teddy Boys' Picnic.

The café flourished, and Kaye was persistently bombarded with requests to remain open after 9pm. The law-abiding businessman patiently explained that he would certainly lose his existing music licence if he acceded to their pleas, and the boys and girls grudgingly went home. Appreciating the fact that Tiverton did not have a youth centre, and aware that both the Constitutional and Liberal Clubs had music playing until 10.30pm, Kaye consulted local solicitor Frank Suter. He informed Kaye that any club would normally be permitted a music licence until at least 10.30pm daily, and 10pm on Sundays.

Eventually the snack bar in West Exe was closed, the premises being purchased by entrepreneur Harry Tidball, and the Kaylee Coffee Club, for members and their invited guests only, was opened at premises in Gold Street, Tiverton, by Kaye and his friend and new business-partner, local photographer Lee Flaws. This club also closed after an extremely successful twelve-month period, when Kaye and Lee were unable to finalise the renting of an adjacent property, which was needed to meet stringent hygiene standards. The little snack bar in West Exe and the Kaylee club are still remembered by many with great affection.

Tiverton's first official centre for youth was opened in 1959, when local councillor and prominent businessman, Henry Ayres, formed a committee with the intention of providing young people with a place in which to relax and enjoy each other's company. The former police station in St Andrew Street was selected for the purpose, and the sea cadet force from TS *Hermes*, under the supervision of their Commanding Officer, Jack Clayton, was press-ganged into decorating the allocated rooms. A coffee bar was constructed, and crockery, tables and seating obtained.

Leonard 'Curly' Harder, a male nurse by profession, ran a coffee bar for the sea cadets at their canal-basin headquarters on training nights, and was offered the position of part-time youth leader at the new youth club. Curly's acceptance was to see him involved with the youth of Tiverton for the next twenty-three years.

Lee Flaws.

COFFEE CLUB

"Kaylee"

21b GOLD STREET, TIVERTON

Subscriptions are
8/- Yearly
5/- Half-yearly

Each member may bring one Guest at a charge of 6d. per evening to comply with Club Rules—copies of which are on view at the Club

Kaylee Coffee Club
membership card.

Twelve 'sugars' and Curly: (L–R back row) *Lorna Salter, Leonard 'Curly' Harder.* (L–R front – maiden names) *Margaret Moyce, ? , Ann Maynard, Camelia Lane, Sue Tibbenham, ? , Pat Pearce, Joyce Hotchkiss, Kate Irwin, Carol Rooks, Kay Pengelly.*

Initially, the club opened between the hours of 7.30pm and 10.30pm on Monday evenings only, entrance to which cost each member a shilling (5p). Curly did not finish work at Tidcombe Hall until 8pm, so his wife Joan opened the centre. The attendance figures very quickly prompted the decision to open on an additional evening, and Thursday night became pop party night.

The pop parties gave local rock bands the opportunity to perform to a live audience. Bands such as The Echoes, The Falcons, The Staccatos and The Avengers all got their first real break at the little club, and the evenings were possibly over-supported. Dancing shoulder-to-shoulder there were often times when a young lady would faint due to the heat. In these instances the girl would be lifted bodily, passed above the heads of the crowd, and taken to an adjoining room to recover. Inevitably, she would be seen dancing ten minutes later, apparently no worse for wear.

Jiving the night away – Curly and Lorna.

Sharing a secret with The Staccatos.

Curly's six-feet-plus frame and imposing presence ensured that the pop parties were largely incident free. The club's caretaker, who lived next door, occasionally complained that his television set 'bounced' each Thursday evening, and the landlord of the Star public house at the top of St Andrew Street noticed that his pub sign had disappeared (a gentleman walking his dog along the canal towpath found it and reported his find to the police), but with these exceptions, there were few problems to speak of.

Like Kaye Holland, Curly steadfastly defended the reputation of his young men and women, and encouraged them to actively participate in events of a benevolent nature. A 15-mile sponsored walk, the result of a challenge to the youth centre from the Tiverton Rugby Football Club, was completed by even the portliest of members. In subsequent and consecutive years, the distance was increased to 25 miles, and then 50 miles (Curly took to his car for this one).

Dances were held at the Heathcoat Hall in Wellbrook Street, Tiverton, both for youth club funds and for local charities and, again, the budding rock stars of the district were able to demonstrate their musical prowess.

♩ ♫ ♪

Regular visits to and from other youth clubs in the Mid Devon area, designed to inculcate a sense of harmony, were important dates in the calendar. The Tiverton club developed a particular affinity with its counterpart at Burnthouse Lane in Exeter, an area that, through the antics of one or two idiots, had gained a reputation for being rough. The courtesy and hospitality shown to the visitors from Tiverton was always creditable. Curly's law upon any such outing stated that, 'There will be no beer and no barrels on the bus.' If the visit was taking place on, or in the vicinity of 5 November, a rider was added, '...and no bangers'.

The lounge bar of the Dolphin.

In February 1963, a coach filled with members of the Tiverton club which included The Avengers pop group, who were to supply the music, travelled down the valley road for an evening of fun and dancing with their friends at Burnthouse Lane. The boys in the band had been playing for an hour or more when the leader of the host club suggested to his heavily-perspiring opposite number, that they nip up to the Dolphin for a swift pint. Looking across a heaving dance floor and assured that the assistant leaders would hold the fort, Curly readily agreed.

Taking but a few moments to reach the public house, the two leaders entered the saloon bar. Curly was horrified to discover that a dozen of his club members had beaten them to it. On noticing their leader, the embarrassed boys and girls from Tiverton put down their glasses and wordlessly left the bar. Anticipating a tongue-lashing when Curly returned, the itinerants were flabbergasted when the matter was neither broached at the club, nor on the homeward bus. Curly did in fact never raise the subject, preferring instead to let the miscreants (the average age of whom

Tiverton Youth Centre in Bolham Road, Tiverton.

was fifteen years) reflect on their wrongdoing. Such was the nature of Curly Harder, the gentle giant.

The little youth club in St Andrew Street closed in 1964, although the building stands today. Curly accepted the post of deputy warden at the new all-purpose centre in Bolham Road, Tiverton, working alongside Brian 'Chugg' Stephenson, the newly appointed warden.

'Book 'em Dan'l'.

Together with David 'Dan'l' Wood, formerly the manager of The Echoes, The Falcons and The Starfires, Curly adhered to his policy of employing local rock groups for dances at the Bolham Road centre whenever possible, and the debt of gratitude owed to him by those musicians is inestimable.

Thus we moved from the skiffle and big-band era, to the heady days of rock and roll. This book has been written firstly as a tribute to the boys and girls who, after countless hours of practice, have entertained not only themselves, but also the people of Tiverton and the Mid Devon area. Secondly it is hoped that it will bring back fond memories of times spent dancing and listening to the music supplied by the district's own 'pop stars'.

For me, it is a collection of treasured memories, some sad, but in the main happy, and I sincerely hope that you will enjoy browsing through the pages that follow.

Barry Sowden
Tiverton
August 2000

A Tribute to Bill Greenhalgh

No book about rock and roll would be complete without reference to William Greenhalgh, his wife Una and daughter Jane, who, with their loyal and knowledgeable staff, ran their excellent music shop(s) in Exeter during the 1950s, 60s and 70s – the central period covered by this book. Sadly, Bill passed away on 6 November 1985, aged seventy-two, but the business continues to flourish with Una and Jane at the helm. From the age of nineteen, for a period of five years, Bill's son Andrew was also integral to the business, assisting his parents and sister in the shops during the day, and carrying out public relations for various bands during the evenings.

Mrs Una Greenhalgh.

Jane Greenhalgh.

Bill purchased the Music Mart at 120 Fore Street, Exeter, from a company called Clarke & Shinn, and traded from these premises for approximately eighteen months, prior to selling the property and moving to 129 Fore Street. The Greenhalgh family later acquired the three properties in Fore Street from which they currently trade, and sold the building situated at 129 which presently houses a fish and chip shop.

Would-be guitarists, drummers, keyboard and brass players flocked to the Music Mart where Bill, an accomplished violinist and saxophonist himself, would dispense advice and encouragement to both the novice and the experienced player.

Young musicians were invariably penniless, but nonetheless desperate to acquire equipment that would provide them with the sound produced by their hit parade heroes. To enable the youngsters to realise their dreams Bill, an astute, but kindly and caring man, devised a form of 'in house' hire-

The shop in Fore Street, Exeter.

purchase agreement, which involved a legal and binding contract coupled with a blue fold-over instalment card, upon which the deposit and subsequent payments were recorded. The agreement required a parental signature where the purchaser was under the age of twenty-one, and it was not unheard of for a musician to tell Bill, 'My father's parked just up the road, I'll pop up and get his signature.' The agreement was returned to the shop a few minutes later, and the chosen instrument handed over. Bill was completely unaware that the young musician's father was currently miles away, and that the resourceful youth had signed his father's name leaning on a nearby shop window!

On Saturdays, a constant stream of musicians would enter the shop, to this day known countywide in musical circles simply as 'Bill's', and offer him £1 or £2, usually in dog-eared £1 notes or occasionally in loose change. The following was typical of a conversation between a musician and our Bill:

Musician: 'Here's a quid Bill, can't afford anymore this week.'
Bill: 'That's not a lot is it?'
Musician: 'I'm a bit skint at the moment – me van's packed up, and I'm lookin' at big money to get it going.'
Bill: 'You're not skint at all! I read in the *Express and Echo* that you were playing at Seaton Town Hall on Friday, the Manor Pavilion in Sidmouth on Saturday, and the '400' Club in Torquay on Sunday – so give us a fiver or you'll never pay the thing off!'

So it was with Bill Greenhalgh. A shrewd businessman and fellow musician, who will be fondly remembered by all who purchased their equipment from the Music Mart.

William 'Bill' Greenhalgh.

The Groups

PART ONE

The Bluebirds: (L–R) Cyril Blackford, Stan 'Bungy' Beer, Derek 'Digger' Ford, Terry Cottrell, Bernard Rewe, John Bryant.

The Bluebirds

Initially a traditional dance trio, The Bluebirds were founded in 1954 by three young men from the Witheridge and District parishes. Friends and former pupils of Chulmleigh school, the line-up was John Bryant, Cyril Blackford and a relative of Cyril's, Derek 'Digger' Ford, the proprietor of the Hare and Hounds Garage in Witheridge.

John and Cyril had played the accordion for some time, John gaining valuable experience by sitting in with Cyril who was formerly a member of a band called The Rhythm Songsters. Digger had for some time fancied playing the drums, and it was due to his offer to buy a set of drums, and provide the transportation to and from dances, that The Bluebirds were formed. Digger's first kit, which included the most enormous bass drum, was duly purchased from Don Bowles' shop at Angel Hill in Tiverton, and the band began rehearsing with a will. The band needed a name, of course, and this too was provided by Digger, who had given slightly more than a fleeting glance to a famous toffee wrapper, the prior contents of which he was currently enjoying.

OPEN FOR ENGAGEMENTS

BLUE BIRD DANCE BAND

'Phone :
Witheridge 203

D. J. Ford,
12, Butts Close,
Witheridge,
Tiverton.

Wanna book The Bluebirds?

The regular weekend dances, and the annual hunt ball, usually held in the village hall, were eagerly awaited, well supported on the night, and were an integral part of the community's social life. The relatively small number of bands playing strict-tempo music, compared with the number of villages in need of their talents, meant that The Bluebirds were always in demand. Subsequently, clarinetist Terry Cottrell, was 'imported' from Tiverton to give the band an extra dimension, to be followed some six months later by local man Stanley 'Bungy' Beer, a driver with the Devon General Bus Company, who played the double bass. Additionally, saxophonist Bernard Rewe could be relied upon to augment the band when, as John Bryant used to say, 'Us needed the full orchestra'. Bernard was also largely responsible for Terry's transition to alto-saxophone from clarinet.

Extra rehearsals were necessary to allow the new members of the band to familiarise themselves with the music. These practices were held at the home of John's mum and dad, in North Street, Witheridge. It was at one of these sessions, when Stan Beer was imitating the double-bass player with Bill Haley's Comets by spinning the instrument through 360 degrees, that Mrs Bryant noticed with horror that the metal spike on the bottom of the bass had neatly drilled a hole in a new fireside rug, was relentlessly continuing through the linoleum below, and was about to create a pattern on her front-room floor. Fortunately, unlike his hysterical wife, Mr Bryant could see the funny

Austin 6, one of Digger's Ford Fleet, being put to more conventional use than lugging Bluebirds and equipment.

side of things, and resolved the situation by placing a saucer, normally reserved for the cat, under the offending spike.

On another occasion, en route to a dance at Hawkridge, a pretty village on Exmoor, four members of the band in a Morris Eight, part of Digger's fleet of taxis, and the selected transport for the evening, encountered Slate Hill, the gradient of which was not dissimilar to the one which has made Porlock famous.

With the massive bass firmly anchored to the roof with baler twine, the equally large bass drum secured to the drop down boot-lid in the same fashion, four passengers – all, with exception of the driver, carrying accordions and such-like as hand luggage – the vehicle flatly refused to comply with Digger's plaintive request of, 'Come on Maid, you can do it.'

Undeterred, and showing commendable regard for their waiting audience, the four musicians disembarked, unloaded the instruments and carried them to the top of the hill. Digger then returned to the vehicle and drove it up the hill, where the instruments were reloaded. The band then continued nonchalantly on their way.

In 1959 John Bryant was called upon to serve Queen and Country, through National Service. The band was fortunate, however, in that experienced cover was available. Accordionist Peter Boax proved to be an ideal replacement, his love of music, personality and playing style fitting the bill perfectly.

In the twelve months following John's departure, both Terry Cottrell and Stan Beer left the band to pursue other interests. Despite the fact that The Bluebirds were now a trio, they continued to delight audiences throughout the district with their humour and their music, well into the 1960s.

The Chekkers

When Mr and Mrs Dray gave their son John a guitar as a birthday present it was with severe misgivings and, as it transpired, well-founded trepidation. A pupil at the Tiverton Grammar School, John, though somewhat introverted, was a popular and intelligent boy who enjoyed his studies. His parents fostered the hope that he would be successful academically, and perhaps enter the world of business and commerce rather than playing in one of those 'blasted beat groups'.

About a year later, whilst playing his guitar in the garden of the family home in Hazel Lane, Rewe, the postman arrived. He informed John that a lad who had just moved into the nearby Triangle Garage (now known as Speedway Garage) also played the guitar. Wasting no time, John contacted the garage, spoke to the new proprietor Mr Crozier, and was soon introduced to his son Geoffrey. Striking up an instant friendship, John was delighted to learn that he and his new-found friend would be attending the same school, and almost in tears when he heard Geoff play his guitar. It was evident even to his untrained ear that Geoff was light-years ahead both in technique and chord knowledge. From that moment on the two boys would play their guitars together at every opportunity, Geoff skilfully picking out the melody, with John strumming the chords and singing. The year was 1959, and Mr and Mrs Dray's 'worst nightmare' had begun.

School friends Jack Cooper and Chris 'Kipper' Tree were recruited as drummer and reserve rhythm guitarist respectively, together with Jeff Horrell,

Rehearsing at Speedway Garage: (L–R) Geoff Crozier, Chris 'Kipper' Tree, Jack Cooper, John Dray and Jeff Horrell.

The Chekkers play al fresco at Tiverton Grammar School.

a pal from Stoke Canon on tea-chest bass. Thus The Coyotes skiffle group came into being. Practices were held in the restaurant at the Triangle Garage, and patrons were often serenaded while dining; a sort of 'beat while you eat'.

The year 1960 was one of transformation. The band changed its name to The Chekkers (the imaginative spelling courtesy of Jack Cooper), dispensed with skiffle in favour of rock and roll, and went 'fully electric' by fitting John's Hohner acoustic (untuneable above the fifth fret) with a pick-up, and by the purchase of a small amplifier. The occasionally over-enthusiastic Jack upgraded his drum kit, and Jeff's visit to Bill Greenhalgh's music emporium in Exeter proved productive when he obtained a neck section from a double bass, which appeared to have been in a road-traffic accident. Remarkably, he later built a wooden body for the instrument which in essence looked and sounded quite good.

The boys ready to rock with their Rolls Royce Landaulet.

Regular rehearsal under the musical directorship of Geoff Crozier yielded results. The band was asked to play at the Three Tuns public house in Silverton, and other bookings quickly followed. The surge in popularity, flattering as it was, gave rise to a major problem: how to transport musicians and equipment to functions? Jeff Horrell was to provide the solution.

He loved to tinker with engines, and had a special interest in ancient vehicles of any kind, including motorcycles and tractors. Learning of an apparently abandoned vehicle in a caravan park at the top of Telegraph Hill, near Exeter, he borrowed his father's van, drove to the site, and was almost euphoric on discovering that the vehicle in question was a 1928 Rolls Royce. The owner was quickly located and the car purchased for the sum of £40 (about one

'Like our new gear?': (L–R) John Dray, Geoff Crozier, Jeff Horrell, Jack Cooper.

month's wages). Jeff later returned with a foot pump to inflate the tyres, a battery, some petrol and an insurance cover note, and was amazed some four hours later to hear the motor burst into life. Back at the family farm, Jeff practically rebuilt the rear end of the Rolls out of plywood, and silenced a noisy exhaust with parts from an International tractor. For many months this lovingly 'hand-crafted' example of British engineering at its finest (discounting the Horrell modifications), was in constant use as The Chekkers' 'executive transport'.

During the same period, Jeff, in an attempt to keep up with the 'increasingly-electric' Chekkers, purchased a blue-green Rosetti bass guitar. When he was unavailable for a gig (normally during the summer months), local musician, Brian Nott, would stand in. From the outset, it was quite obvious that Brian was by far the better bass player, and he fitted in well with Geoff, John and Jack. These indisputable facts were honourably acknowledged by Jeff Horrell, who suggested that Brian join the group on a permanent basis, whilst he would act as the band's driver and 'roadie'.

Belting out 'Flycatcher' at Halberton Village Hall.

This amicable arrangement continued until the end of 1960 when a series of events caused the demise of the band. Geoff Crozier moved to Kingswear, near Dartmouth, to study building design at Torquay Technical College, where a local band called the Rockfellas soon snapped up his guitar-playing talents.

Jack Cooper moved to Porthcurnow in Cornwall to attend the Cable & Wireless Training Centre, and did not play again for several years.

John Dray began a career in banking with the National Provincial Bank in Cullompton, necessitating a move into 'digs' there. During the time he spent in Cullompton he entered and won the Billy Wheeler talent contest, held at the Assembly Rooms, beating Hawaiian guitarist Martin Blythe into second place. John subsequently joined the Ottery St Mary-based Cyclones as their rhythm guitarist.

John Dray.

Brian Nott.

Brian Nott pursued his chosen career in electronics with Stenner Ltd of Tiverton, in addition to a busy, five-nights-a-week schedule working with Vic Palmer's dance combo, before linking with Dave Walker as a member of the very successful Falcons.

Jeff Horrell became fully committed to the farm and the family business and, having no further need for the Rolls Royce, part-exchanged it for a Ford Squire van and £80 in cash. The Rolls Royce is currently owned by a businessman in Holland and believed to be worth an estimated £40 000!

'Kipper' Tree had long since ceased to be a playing member of The Chekkers, but was to reappear on the local music scene with The Thunderbirds.

In 1965, Geoff Crozier, John Dray, Brian Nott and Jack Cooper met at the House of Sound studio in Bristol, and recorded an extended-play vinyl disc for old times' sake. The EP featured four instrumentals – 'Wail', 'Big Chief Whoopin' Koff', 'Yellow Jacket', and a tune written by Geoff Crozier called 'Flycatcher'. Recorded out of sheer sentimentality, the disc sold seven copies. (John Dray says he bought three of them!)

There can be little doubt that The Chekkers made a significant contribution to the local music scene in those early days, and doubtless this is due in no small way to the powerful and innovative guitar playing of Geoff Crozier. Still held in high esteem by those of us who were fortunate enough to hear him play, Geoff must have done a lot for the sales of the Hofner Futurama guitar in the South West.

The Chekkers are still regularly in touch with each other, and one cannot help wondering when the strains of 'Flycatcher' will be heard in Tiverton once more.

The Strollers also known as Johnny and the Strollers

In the almost forty years' period since the dissolution of The Strollers, there has been much conjecture as to why arguably the most popular local band of the early 1960s ceased to be. It is my intention that this biography should become the definitive work on the subject.

In 1960, his three years in the RAF over, John Whitter returned to Tiverton and secured employment with John Heathcoat & Company. Prior to his National Service he had been a member of The Duffels skiffle group, and was anxious to get involved in the local music scene once again.

Musicians were then, as now, a gregarious bunch that wanted simply to make music – and not testosterone-fuelled egotists, as was the belief of many.

John 'Tex' Whitter.

Vince Beer.

Paul 'Wig' Irwin.

Colin 'Snare' Roberts.

Members of 'rival' bands, like itinerant minstrels would meet, hold 'jam sessions' and practise, merely because they loved to play or sing. These bedouin tendencies, coupled with fading memories, has made it difficult to positively identify all of the musicians who accompanied John prior to the formation of The Strollers proper. Nevertheless, it is known that guitarists Gordon 'Tubby' Hurford, when on weekend leave from the RAF, and another ex-Duffel, Peter White, lent their talents to John's exceptional voice.

Doubtless, the first line-up and the one that will be best remembered by the band's many fans, was that of Johnny handling vocals and playing rhythm guitar, lead guitarist Vince Beer, Paul 'Wig' Irwin on bass guitar, and drummer Colin 'Snare' Roberts.

Research into the musical background of the four lads reveals that, as mentioned earlier, Johnny had previously been a member of a skiffle group – as had Paul Irwin. Vince was the proud owner of a Spanish, round-holed guitar – a present from his Auntie Joan and Uncle Ken Hookway which had been tastefully painted white by well-known violinist and proprietor of an auto refinishing firm, Ron Davey. Colin Roberts had been taught to play the drums by Frank Bond, a colleague at his place of work, W.G. Dunsford, in Bampton Street, Tiverton.

Phillip Main.

Vince Beer had attended an audition at the New Hall in Tiverton and been invited to become the new band's lead guitarist. He subsequently mentioned that Wig, who for some time had hankered to play the bass guitar and often practised at Vince's home, might like to join the band. Colin recounts that he heard that the outfit was looking for a drummer, and sort of 'drifted' into the set-up.

The Strollers were the proverbial overnight sensation. The newly-purchased electric guitars and amplification, not to mention the Swiss echo unit (the first of its type in the South West), enhanced the already smooth sound. Vince's laid-back, but accurate guitar work on instrumental numbers by The Shadows and The Ventures contrasted beautifully with John's vocals.

The band was hugely popular in both local and outlying dance halls. So popular in fact, that three of their most ardent supporters – Mervyn Dawe, and Phillip and his brother David 'Bungy' Main – started a fan club, which at one point boasted over 500 members. Phil further demonstrated his loyalty to the band by becoming its manager, a position that he held throughout The Strollers' heyday.

David 'Bungy' Main.

The younger of the Main brothers, 'Bungy', in addition to being a 'leading light' within The Strollers' fan club, was also a competent guitarist – founding both The Mainliners and The Stormers with fellow guitarist Rob 'Reuben J.' Hayball – but surprisingly, neither of the bands made an impact on the local scene; unlike The Strollers, who had taken the area by storm!

On 19 September 1961, Johnny, Vince, Wig and Colin went into the studios

The Strollers: (L–R) John Whitter, Colin Roberts, Paul Irwin and Vince Beer.

of the Bristol & West Recording Services in Park Row, Bristol. A long and tiring day resulted in the production of two extended-play vinyl discs. Side one on the first disc featured an instrumental penned by lead guitarist Vince Beer called 'Night Walker', and a song called 'In A Mansion'. On the flip side of disc one were another instrumental 'White Silver Sands' and a country and western number 'Jesse James'.

The second EP contained cover versions of two Buddy Holly classics, 'Rave On' and 'Listen to Me', and, keeping to the same format as the first disc, two instrumentals, 'Blue Moon' and the Duane Eddy favourite, 'Forty Miles of Bad Road'. The EPs were distributed by the fan club and sold in profusion.

Sales of the two records and the adulation heaped upon them by their supporters prompted much discussion regarding the feasibility of a trip to Europe. A two-week working holiday was arranged through contacts made by John during his time with the RAF. In the summer of 1962, with the minimum of equipment loaded into the Dormobile, The Strollers travelled to Holland.

The boys were wonderful ambassadors for the West Country, and Tiverton in particular. Playing mainly on American airbases, the band was well received at each of the four or five venues in which they performed, and a recording contract was strongly intimated. The Strollers returned to Tiverton exhausted after their 'holiday', but happy in the knowledge that they had proved themselves.

In their absence, manager Phil Main had been extremely busy, accepting bookings, and hiring coaches to transport the band's supporters to the various functions. Additionally, Phil, in collaboration with Gordon Vearncombe, the owner of the Electric Cinema in Newport Street, Tiverton, had arranged for The Strollers to play during the interval at the première of a new film starring the young actor Ray Brooks.

'Some People': (L–R) *Gordon Vearncombe, John Whitter, Ann Whitter, Ray Brooks, Colin Roberts, Mary Hasnich, Vince Beer and Paul Irwin.*

Colin Webber.

The film entitled *Some People*, was premièred on 8 October 1962, and was seen by many hundreds of people during its run at the Electric. Ray Brooks, an unpretentious and handsome fellow, attended the Tiverton première, signing autograph books and publicity photographs – and more importantly bought The Strollers a round of drinks!

Johnny Whitter, who by this time had left his previous employer and was working at Beeston's music shop in Bampton Street, had for some while harboured a desire to set aside his guitar and concentrate solely upon his singing. Colin Webber, the rhythm guitarist of the highly respected Stringbeats, and 'part-time' apprentice piano tuner with Beestons, was persuaded to join The Strollers, allowing John to develop his stage act unencumbered by the large semi-acoustic.

The mini tour of Holland earlier in the year repeatedly arose in conversation, and the decision was finally taken to accept the challenge of professional musicianship and return once again to the Continent.

John, 'Snare' and Colin Webber immediately quit their employment. 'Wig' asked his employer to grant him extended leave but his request was denied. 'Wig' was, however, permitted to take an early vacation, on completion of which his notice was tendered. Vince Beer, having recently become engaged to be married, and manager Phil Main, who thought the risk too great, parted company with The Strollers at the end of 1962. Martin 'Bugsy' Irwin, Paul's younger brother, became the band's new lead guitarist, and Gordon Vearncombe donned the mantle of manager.

In the spring of 1963, the 'new look' Johnny and the Strollers returned to Holland. Gordon had suggested that the band defer its decision – until the 'English sound' had taken a firmer hold on the European dance scene – but they were not to be dissuaded.

Initially all was well. Johnny was living at the home of his Dutch wife Ann's parents in Roermond, while the two Colins and the Irwin brothers were well cared for by a charming couple, 'Mama and Papa' Kessels, at their house in nearby Swalmen. The Strollers quickly settled into the groove. The earlier suggestion of a recording contract became a reality, with a contract signed, and the band entered the studios of Telstar records. The resulting single – a cover version of Billy Fury's 'I'd Never Find Another You', and its nominal B-side 'Let Him Go, Let Him Tarry'– reached the number-three spot in the Benelux top ten.

In October 1963, the follow-up, 'No, You Can't Say No', backed with 'Worries Worry Me' – both written by Colin Webber and 'Wig' Irwin, and featuring Caesarine, the daughter of record producer Johnny Hoes – also entered the charts, but with less success.

For many months the boys were phenomenally successful, and constantly in demand, performing regularly at the airbase in Brugen in addition to many clubs and hotels, but unfortunately it was not to last. Whether or not the arrival of 'Beatlemania' and the Liverpool Sound into Europe had any bearing on the decrease in The Strollers' popularity can only be surmised, but the boys suddenly found themselves in the unenviable position of being without engagements and finances.

Bye-bye to Blighty: (L–R) *Colin Webber, John Whitter, Colin Roberts, Martin 'Bug' Irwin, 'Wig' Irwin.*

Give it some clog! (L–R, on roof) *Colin Roberts, John Whitter, 'Wig' Irwin. (L–R, standing) Colin Webber, 'Bug' Irwin, Bruce Bonebright – USAF Bases Entertainments Manager.*

31

The situation gradually worsened and, deciding that they had given professional musicianship their best shot, long-serving 'Wig' Irwin and 'Snare' Roberts, together with Colin Webber and 'Bug' Irwin, returned to England penniless, disbanding immediately.

Johnny Whitter remained in Holland, where it is understood that, at the suggestion of record producer Johnny Hoes, he changed his surname to Ramone and formed another band called The Moles. He too eventually returned to England and continued in the music business for many years.

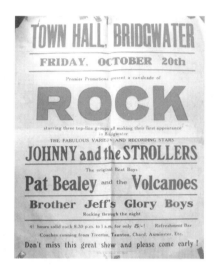

The Cyclones featuring Johnny Carme

The Cyclones: (L–R) Ralph 'Dozy' Dowell, Richard Bagwell, John Vanstone, Reg Bagwell.

Like The Stringbeats, The Cyclones did not originate in the Mid Devon area, but, as will be apparent later in this biography, they had strong links with Tiverton and its surrounding district.

Formed in the late 1950s by the very talented Bagwell brothers, Reg and Richard, the lead and bass guitarists respectively, they were joined by rhythm guitarist Peter Bavington and drummer Ralph 'Dozy' Dowel. Lead vocalist John Vanstone, who adopted the stage name Johnny Carme, completed the traditional line-up. In addition, a singer called Carol Leask from Sidmouth, in East Devon, occasionally augmented the band.

Beauty and the Beast: Carol Holland (née Leask) and John Dray.

The older of the two Bagwells by one year, and heavily influenced by both skiffle and the wave of rock and roll at this time sweeping the UK, Reg had studied guitar at the Exeter School of Music. Younger brother Richard had been taught to play the tenor banjo by a Mr Rhangatan, at St Luke's teacher-training college, also in Exeter. The staff of Devon Lady Ltd, the manufacturers of sectional buildings based at Honiton, became accustomed to the sight of their colleague slinging the banjo around his shoulders, mounting his motorcycle and riding off to his weekly lesson. Whilst Richard's musical taste leaned toward traditional jazz, he shared his brother's love of music generally.

Peter Bavington owned an electric guitar and small 'training' amplifier, and was a regular visitor to the Bagwell household in the hamlet of Alfington, near Ottery St Mary, living as he did, just three doors away. Drummer Ralph

The Cyclones: (L–R) Tony Solman, Richard Bagwell, Pete Bavington, Reg Bagwell.

Dowel affectionately, if somewhat unfortunately, nicknamed Dozy, had purchased his kit from Bill Greenhalgh's music store, and Reg, Richard and Peter all vividly remember the 36" (approximately 915mm) diameter, riveted Zildjan cymbal which formed part of the kit. Throughout the day following each and every booking, all three boys would suffer from a mild form of tinnitus (ringing in the ears).

Johnny Carme, with a laudable regard for his vocal chords, included in his diet a well-known brand of sweet, which from its name could have been produced specifically for musicians, but in any case they allegedly helped one to breathe more easily!

Reg and Richard were remarkable in being, as they were, equally adept lead or bass guitarists, and often exchanged roles (an imaginative highlight of any stage act, but a nightmare for an author trying to identify the similarly featured brothers from a publicity photograph). In truth, the Bagwells' acquisition of electric guitars and amplification coupled with solid rehearsal, led to The Cyclones' formation and rapid rise in status to semi-professionalism, Reg usually playing lead guitar, with brother Richard on bass.

The Cyclones: (L–R) Reg Bagwell, Tony Solman, John Vanstone (aka Johnny Carme), John Dray and Richard Bagwell.

There can be few town and village halls in East and Mid Devon, whose boards were not graced by the band and, as their popularity increased, the outfit could also be seen in South Devon and Somerset.

Pete Bavington became an ex-Cyclone, for reasons undisclosed, in 1963, and was replaced by John Dray. Previously the rhythm guitarist and vocalist with The Chekkers, John had been sitting on the doorstep of a popular music shop in Exeter 'road testing' a guitar, and had been asked by Reg Bagwell if he was currently playing with a band. Receiving a reply in the negative, Reg had invited him to join The Cyclones and the offer was accepted.

The single other change in personnel resulted from Ralph Dowel's relocation to another area by his employer. Tony Solman, once a drummer in the Boys' Brigade, requested that he be given an opportunity to play with the band, and proved to be both capable and compatible with the other members of The Cyclones. Together with John Dray, Tony provides the 'local' link essential for inclusion in this book, as mentioned at the start of this biography.

A very successful period ensued, with manager Ken Stiling working hard on the band's behalf. Entered by him in a talent competition held at the Civic Hall in Exeter to find the area's top band, The Cyclones were, perhaps predictably, beaten into second place by The Stringbeats, two members of which group desperately wanted to turn professional. Some weeks later at a dance in the Town Hall at Dulverton, featuring both The Cyclones and The Stringbeats, the two gentlemen in question, namely lead guitarist Brian Wright and bass player John Phripp, approached John Dray and Tony Solman and suggested that they join them in becoming professional musicians.

Initial rehearsals went extremely well but, due to family and career problems, John Dray relinquished all further thought of earning a living from music. Not so Tony Solman, whose career details from this point are to be found in The Stringbeats' biography, later in this book.

After The Cyclones' split, Reg and Richard Bagwell drafted organist Pete Adey, and the former drummer with The Midnight Blues, from Exmouth, Stuart Clarke, into the band, now named The Reason Why, but were with the band for a short time only. A number of different drummers followed Stuart Clarke. Alan Williams, Howard Clarke and Stuart Tuckett all played during the consolidation period.

The combination of Reg, Richard and, from Exeter, drummer Steve Mercer, now collectively known as Freeway, once again broke into the top flight of the semi-professional scene. The stress and pressures created by the management of their own businesses, allied with a busy musical schedule, finally became inhibitive, and Freeway disbanded in the early 1990s.

The Stringbeats Also known as The Vampires, The Variations and The Academy

Above: The Vampires: (L–R) Mike Herniman, Colin Webber, John Phripp and Brian Wright.

Right: The Stringbeats: (L–R) Mike Herniman, Colin Webber, John Phripp, Brian Wright and Brian Barnett.

Whilst this book is essentially devoted to bands from Tiverton and the surrounding parishes, it would be at the very least remiss, and at most unforgivable, to omit The Stringbeats. The author makes no apologies for their inclusion.

Like so many teenagers in the late 1950s, John Hillier, from the hamlet of Brushford, near Dulverton in Somerset, played the guitar for his own, and that of his singing friend John Phripp's, amusement. Usually referred to as J.J., the initials of his Christian names, John Phripp later acquired a six-string Spanish guitar and would pick out the bass line as instructed by John H. Mutual friend Brian Wright who, like J.J., lived at Exebridge, joined them at their rehearsals with his guitar, a present from enthusiastic parents Sid and Susie (their enthusiasm was to wane in the years that lay ahead when they realised that youngest son Brian was apparently nocturnal).

The practice band became a four-piece when Roger Mackney, whose parents owned a draper's shop in Dulverton, joined for a short time as their singer. The traditional three guitars, drums and vocalist line-up was completed by the addition of former Dulverton Town Band drummer, Mike Herniman. In 1960 Messrs Hillier, Phripp, Wright and Herniman went 'live' for the first time. Calling themselves The Vampires, the boys provided free entertainment for the end-of-term dance at Dulverton Secondary Modern School.

When John Hillier left the band twelve months later, Brian adopted the role of lead guitarist and Colin Webber, an apprentice piano tuner from nearby Bampton, was recruited to play rhythm guitar.

By 1962 The Vampires had changed their name to The Stringbeats and were managed by Albert Harvey. They now featured new front-man, Brian

Barnett, who lived across the border in Loxbeare, Devon. Brian had been selected from several hopefuls who had auditioned, and he sang with the band for about a year before leaving the area.

The Stringbeats were by this time an extremely marketable product. They had long since acquired new guitars, drums, microphones, amplification and so on, courtesy of hire purchase and Bill Greenhalgh's music emporium in Exeter, and had developed a style and technique unique to the area – through constant attention to detail at their weekly rehearsals. Their professional approach in a semi-professional world brought a great deal of respect and admiration from their ardent supporters and other musicians.

Invariably when a band becomes moderately successful, one member for whatever reason chooses that moment to leave. Johnny Whitter, a fellow employee of Beestons in Bampton Street, Tiverton, persuaded Colin Webber to join his band, The Strollers. Colin's last duty as a member of The Stringbeats, before going to Holland with his new band, was to inform Albert Harvey that he no longer figured in the long-term plans of the group.

Dulverton teenager Richard 'Rick' Gray accepted an invitation to become the band's rhythm guitarist, in so doing completely disregarding the ministrations of his concerned parents. Newly-appointed manager, Roger Dixie who, like Colin Webber, lived in Bampton, was proving to be first rate in the public relations department, and the band found itself working on three or four evenings of each week. Former Falcons vocalist Mervyn 'Smudge' Gratton lent his talents to The Stringbeats for a period of six months during 1963, but left in the same year.

Following Mervyn's departure, it was decided to collectively shoulder the responsibility for the vocals. There were at the time few bands able to master the complexities of four-part harmony, but the accuracy of Brian's falsetto,

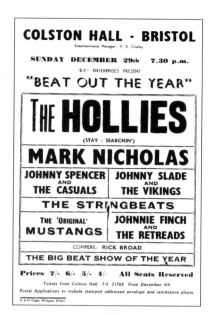

The Stringbeats: (L–R) Mike Herniman, Richard 'Rick' Gray, John Phripp and Brian Wright.

And 'Smudger' makes five! The band, featuring Mervyn 'Smudge' Gratton.

complemented by the voices of John, Mike and Rick, allowed The Stringbeats to cover songs by The Beach Boys and The Four Seasons, with consummate ease.

It was due to the combination of vocal dexterity, Brian Wright's amazing guitar skills, and the all-round cohesion achieved by many hours of practice that, in 1964, The Stringbeats won a talent contest held in the Civic Hall, Exeter. Placed in first position ahead of dozens of other outfits, the band was rewarded with the offer of a sixteen-week season as resident band at Pontin's holiday camp in Paignton, South Devon.

During the week following the audition, the boys, together with manager Roger Dixie, held a meeting to discuss the implications of their success. The four were as one in concluding that they would have to turn professional. The Pontin's contract stipulated that they would be employed

'We are the Champions…'

as bluecoats, the camp hosts engaged to assist and generally entertain the holiday-makers.

Good evening Campers.

Brian, John and Mike were all in the employ of Stenner Ltd; a company based in Lowman Green, Tiverton and part of the Lowman Engineering Group. John, having completed his apprenticeship, decided to throw caution to the wind and become a professional musician, as did Brian who had long harboured a desire to earn a living with his guitar. Young Rick Gray, with GCE (General Certificate of Education) examinations looming large, and with his parents' comments about 'getting a proper job' ringing in his ears, reluctantly left the band. Mike Herniman, with six months of his apprenticeship outstanding, asked if the decision to turn pro could be deferred for that amount of time. Reference was made to the Pontin contract, and Mike was informed that his request was not possible. After careful consideration, Mike opted to remain with his employer and complete his apprenticeship.

Formerly with a band based in Sidmouth, East Devon, called The Cyclones, brilliant young drummer, Tony Solman, subsequently joined Brian and John in founding the area's newest professional outfit. Ironically, The Cyclones gained second place in the aforementioned talent competition. The three lads were duly inducted as bluecoats prior to the start of the summer season and soon adapted to their new lifestyle.

John Phripp was apprehensive when he was instructed to report to the camp office, and a bundle of nerves when he was ushered into the presence of Mrs Pontin, the wife of camp owner Sir Fred. John was asked to take part in a promotional film extolling the virtues of the 'baby listening service' available on the camp. John's part in the film required him to enter a chalet, gaze tenderly at a slumbering infant, and quietly retire. The gentleman engaged to play the role of the child's father, a Mr Ward, was a great fan of The Stringbeats, and when on holiday would listen to their music at every opportunity. From London, a director of Leyton Orient Football Club and an estate agent, Mr Ward suggested to the boys that on completion of their existing contract they move to the capital, where their act could be showcased. In addition, he offered to provide accommodation, act as the band's London agent, and try to secure a recording contract.

Consequently The Stringbeats left the comparative peace of the English Riviera for the hustle and bustle of London, where they were billeted in a property belonging to Leyton Orient FC. Their benefactor, true to his word, worked tirelessly on the band's behalf, and did indeed arrange a recording session. The boys duly attended the studios of Immediate Records, owned by the former manager of The Rolling Stones, Andrew Loog Oldham, and 'laid' several demo tracks.

Shortly after the demo session, drummer Tony Solman announced that it was his intention to return to the West Country and enlist in the Royal Navy. Brian and J.J. tried without success to find a competent drummer to replace

The Variations.

'The Man with All the Toys'.

Tony, and they too found themselves on the A303 heading west. The Stringbeats were effectively no more. Roger Dixie, with no band to manage, decided to devote himself to 'a proper job'.

Back in familiar territory, Brian and John were informed that an Exeter band called The Mustangs were in turmoil, having lost their bass and rhythm guitarists. Contact was established with The Mustangs' vocalist, John Orton (stage name Johnny Cordell), and drummer Dave Cox, both of whom eagerly joined the two ex-Stringbeats to form The Variations.

Sheer unadulterated class! Such comments came from the mouths of fellow musicians (including the writer). The Variations were a superb act. A four-week tour of Germany, which included performances in cities like Brunswick and Hanover, was completed to rave reviews.

The demonstration tracks recorded by The Stringbeats had by this time been carefully scrutinised by the studio producer at Immediate Records, who liked what he had heard. Brian and John subsequently revisited the studio with the 'new boys' to record a song called 'The Man with All the Toys'. Columnist Virginia Ironside reviewed the resulting disc in the *Daily Mail* on Saturday 11 December 1965, as follows: 'Don't be put off by the coy title. It's a really good record with a nice gimmicky backing full of piping "ohs".'

The B-side, penned by lead guitarist, Brian Wright, and entitled 'She'll Know I'm Sorry', was, in the opinion of many, a far superior song, but many thousands were captivated by 'The Toys'.

In an attempt to acquire a bigger sound, organist Graham Parker was drafted into the band. He was, however, soon to be replaced by rhythm guitarist, Robin Sadler. John Phripp was not convinced that the 'heavier style' which the band had adopted suited him and amicably left, his place being taken by bassist Robin Matthews. In the months that were to follow, John set up his highly popular discotheque, Clydisco Mill.

Brian, John Orton and the two Robins continued to perform under the name The Academy but the band was short lived. Thankfully, Brian Wright was to continue playing with a band called Freshwater. The band comprised Brian on lead guitar, Ben Rogers from London on rhythm guitar, former Nashville Skyline drummer Gerry Orchard, and Johnny Ramone. Johnny describes the band as 'the finest I ever worked with'. High praise indeed.

♩ ♫ ♪

The Tuxedos Also known as The Confederates

Doris and Albert Walker were, by the middle of the 1950s, certain that their lives would never be quite the same. The parents of the original Walker brothers, they had purchased a guitar as a birthday present for the second-eldest of their three sons John. Eldest son David played the drums with the Tiverton Youth Orchestra – and it seemed to them that their only hope of leading a normal life lay in youngest son Peter who had, to date, expressed no desire to play any musical instrument.

John, who because of his hair colouring would forever be known as Ginger, learned to play the guitar with the assistance of a teach-yourself book. The careful study of highly-respected guitarist Gordon 'Tubby' Hurford's left

Gordon 'Tubby' Hurford.

The Tuxedos: (from the top) Dave Walker, Ginger Walker, Mervyn Rainey, Paul Midgeley and Alan Ferris.

hand, whenever he performed in the Tiverton area with The Duffels skiffle group, also provided invaluable information. Watching and listening to his younger brother strumming and picking out melodies, David too was smitten with the desire to play the guitar, and eventually purchased his own.

Both employed by John Heathcoat & Company, Ginger and fellow guitarist Paul Midgeley often discussed music during the working day, and when Alan Ferris, an old friend from their school days called at the Walker household and heard David and Ginger play, he offered to play drums, and the formation of a band was inevitable.

Paul, a self-confessed Shadows nut who could play many of their hits note-for-note, was unanimously elected as lead guitarist, and David became the group's rhythm guitarist. During a period that spanned several months, Alan purchased individual drums and cymbals until he had 'built' an adequate, although unmatched, full kit. Ginger's persistent requests for his father's signature on the hire-purchase agreement, which would allow him to acquire a bass guitar, finally paid off, and it was from the Dallas 'Tuxedo' bass that the band got its name.

Practice sessions were invariably held at St Paul's church rooms, Tiverton, and the band reaped its reward from Paul's affection for the music of The Shadows. The boys were, however, unable to increase their repertoire to any degree without a vocalist, and this situation was resolved when Mervyn Rainey was added to The Tuxedos' ranks. With his signature tune 'A Whole Lotta Woman', originally recorded by the somewhat similarly named Marvin Rainwater, Merv gave the band an extra dimension.

Dance promoters requiring the 'dubious sounds' of rock and roll were few, and bookings were sparse, but The Tuxedos could occasionally be heard 'live' at Halberton, Willand and one or two other halls in outlying villages. Although the band was in existence for only a short time, the experience gained from rehearsals and live performances served to act as a springboard to bigger and better things, Merv Rainey, being the sole member not to pursue a semi-professional, or professional career in the field of entertainment.

It is believed that in the years that followed, Albert and Doris Walker became almost resigned to the fact that rock and roll had arrived, and had just a sneaking admiration for their two elder sons' achievements.

♩ ♪♪ ♪

The Echoes

At the time of writing, more than forty years have elapsed since the formation of The Echoes. Memories have faded, research has been difficult, and the resulting biography brief. It is, however, important that the band is featured within this book if only to qualify statements made, and to clarify the interaction between bands.

Probably best described as a practice band, Peter White and Bob Grabham established the outfit in the very early 1960s. Formerly members of The Duffels skiffle group, they were joined by two friends in the employ of John Heathcoat & Company Ltd, Paul Midgeley and John 'Ginger' Walker.

Together with Dave Walker and drummer Alan Ferris, Paul and Ginger had previously been guitarists with the short-lived Tuxedos. Fraternal rivalry, or possibly just the desire for a change may have been the reason why Ginger and his brother, Dave, decided to join different bands – David co-founding The Falcons, and Ginger teaming up once more with Paul, in The Echoes.

Weekly rehearsals were enjoyable and eagerly awaited. All four musicians had gained valuable experience with their previous band or bands, and this

The Echoes at the Heathcoat Hall, Tiverton: (L–R) Bob Grabham, Peter White, Ginger Walker and Paul Midgeley.

'Rocking' Ray Brown.

made the compilation of a comprehensive playlist a formality. The repertoire was further enhanced by the recruitment of 'Rocking' Ray Brown.

Ray Brown had recently moved into the area and had also secured a position with John Heathcoat & Company. Wishing to involve himself with local activities, he became a member of the Signpost Club, and featured in their current production. In the course of his daily toil Ray was introduced to Ginger Walker. He subsequently met Paul, and was invited to join The Echoes as lead vocalist.

The band now lacked just one vital ingredient in their quest for local recognition – bookings! In an effort to remove the aversion to rock and roll harboured by some club secretaries and dance promoters, David 'Dan'l' Wood was approached by Ginger Walker on The Echoes' behalf, and asked to become the band's manager. His protestations that he was not suitably qualified were completely ignored, and he started on a learning curve that would see him manage not one band, but three!

Drawing on his close liaison with Curly Harder at the club in St Andrew Street, Dan'l's answer to the club secretary's preference for old-time, and ballroom dancing, seemed remarkably simple: 'If they won't come to us, then we'll go to them.'

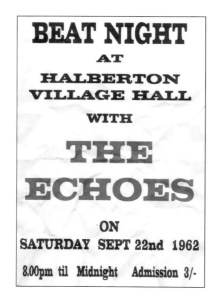

The band booked halls, arranged adequate door stewarding, and sold tickets at the door. On completion of the band's performance, the takings would be counted, and the caretaker of the hall and door stewards located and paid. The remaining monies (if any) were shared equally between the members of the band.

These self-booked dances were, in the main, very enjoyable evenings with few problems. At one such dance however this was not the case. The

Was that an echo?

Echoes travelled to Washfield Village Hall in the Hillman Husky estate car owned by drummer Bob Grabham. The caretaker met them on their arrival and indicated a spot in the small, empty car park adjacent to the hall, where the vehicle was to be parked after the equipment had been unloaded. Always immaculately dressed, and genial, Bob acknowledged the instruction with a cheery, 'right ho'.

The gear was transferred to the stage, and the Hillman parked in the appointed place. Bob had only just begun to remove his drums from their protective cases when a gentleman entered the hall and asked him to move his car. 'I'll be right there,' replied Bob, and duly complied with the request.

Within the space of fifteen minutes, Bob was asked to reposition his car no less than four times. On the fourth occasion, the normally mild-mannered drummer who had yet to complete the setting-up of his kit, turned to his colleagues in the band and said, 'I've moved the car three times already, and enough is enough, I'm off you!'

Without another word, Bob stowed the few items he had managed to unpack when not moving his car, loaded them into the aforementioned vehicle and went home.

A British Leyland Mini, complete with driver, was commandeered, and Dan'l was despatched to Tiverton to fetch drummer Brian Kingdon who, The Echoes felt, would be able to help out. It proved to be so. The harassed manager of The Echoes, the 'hijacked' driver, and a freshly-showered Brian, complete with a snare drum, sticks, one cymbal and two stands, returned to Washfield, and the evening passed without further incident.

Homespun events such as these, played a big part in persuading dance organisers that rock and roll was definitely here to stay, and they grudgingly began to mellow.

The Echoes appeared at most of the village halls in the Tiverton and district area, and periodically ventured across the border. On one particularly memorable Saturday night in 1962 when performing at The Blue Lagoon in Wellington, Somerset, a disagreement between rival gangs escalated into a full-scale punch-up. The police were called, the troublemakers ejected, and order was restored.

The dance hall, however, resembled a saloon bar in downtown Dodge City on the morning after the ranch hands from The Bar 'T', and their sworn enemies from The Lazy 'H', had chosen the same evening and venue in which to spend their round-up bonus. Throughout the fracas The Echoes, from time to time dodging bottles and side-stepping chairs in a manner that would have done justice to a Welsh stand-off half, played on.

On 31 December in the same year, The Echoes were playing at the Heathcoat Hall for the Whitbread Brewery employees' New Year's party. It seemed initially that the 'revellers' were still recovering from the Christmas festivities, and their reticence to dance was frustrating to the boys in the band. The Echoes had been playing to a packed hall with a deserted dance floor for almost an hour. Bob Grabham, concerned that he was not earning his share of the 11 guineas fee, rose from behind his drums, walked to the centre of the stage, grabbed the microphone and sternly told the audience: 'Now listen, no one is dancing and we're wasting our time, if you don't start dancing we may as well pack up and go home!' From the very next, to the very last number, the dance floor was full.

Bob's words regarding 'packing-up' were strangely prophetic. Early in the New Year, Paul left The Echoes to join an Exeter band called The Nightlights, and Ginger became a member of The Starfires. Peter White and Bob Grabham, together with organist Bill Crocker and saxophonist Phil Snell, formed a dance combo called the Music Messengers.

♪ ♫ ♪

The Falcons

All things bright and musical, guitarists great and small,
Don't forget some extra strings, 'cos Dave will break them all.

Sung to the tune of 'All things bright and beautiful', with lyrics by Mr and Mrs Sowden's eldest.

The Falcons beat group comprised: Dave Walker, drummer Alan Ferris, bass player Brian Nott previously with The Chekkers, and more recently although briefly The Staccatos; and Martin Irwin.   The band, fondly if somewhat familiarly christened 'Crockey and Co' by Messrs Sowden, Pope, Bulley and Knowles (collectively known as The Avengers), was formed following the break up of The Tuxedos.

Dave Walker, a bricklayer by trade, was given the nickname 'Crockey' by his fellow workers at Frank Colman & Company, a small building firm from Chettiscombe, near Tiverton. The name evolved over a period of months, starting with Davy, then Davy Crockett, and finally Crockey. It was the considered opinion of many, that Dave sometimes failed to remember that

The Falcons: (L–R) *Dave Walker, Brian Nott, Alan Ferris and Martin 'Bug' Irwin.*

he was holding a plectrum in his right hand and not a builder's trowel, hence the adaptation of the much-loved hymn at the top of this biography. Nevertheless, the speed with which his right hand moved during the playing of some instrumentals, more than compensated for its sledgehammer tendencies.

Lead guitarist Martin 'Bugsy' Irwin, younger brother of The Strollers' bass player, Paul, had 'depped' with several outfits, and was well known by the other members of The Falcons.

Alan 'Rip van Winkle' Ferris, and Brian 'Gungy' Nott had both been members of The Staccatos, a hybrid band with Ginger Walker and the brilliant Geoff Crozier. When Geoff moved to the Bristol area, Ginger decided to join Pete White's Echoes – Alan and Brian choosing to team up with Ginger's elder brother Dave. Merv 'Smudger' Gratton was added to the band shortly after its formation providing an instrumental or vocal option.

Alan Ferris's nickname resulted from an incident following a dance at Willand. The equipment had been loaded – the drums occupying their usual position on the roof rack – and the boys had settled down for the short journey back to Tiverton. Alan was comatose within minutes, and heard neither Bug nor Brian disembark at their respective homes in Halberton. On arriving at Alan's abode, Dan'l Wood, manager of both The Falcons and The Echoes, awakened the slumbering drummer with the words, 'Oy Sleepy, yer 'ome'.

Still drowsy, Alan stepped from the Dormobile and prepared to climb on to its roof with the intention of unloading his drums. The sight of an empty roof rack dispelled his somnolence. The drums were found undamaged, adorning hedgerows and grass verges at various locations between Tiverton and Halberton.

The Falcons flying high at the Heathcoat Hall.

Under the same management, and with the Walker connection, it was perhaps inevitable that the rivalry between The Falcons and The Echoes should be intense. Whether the raw sound produced by The Falcons edged the more melodious Echoes, or the fact that Ginger Walker had not yet begun to sing the lead vocal line, for whatever reason The Falcons seemed to become established, breaking on to the Exeter scene far quicker than their stablemates.

Late, around midnight, on a bleak Saturday in February 1962, The Falcons had just completed a very enjoyable performance at the Civic Hall in Exeter. It had been snowing heavily and the lads decided to take the old A38 route back to Tiverton, via Cullompton, thus avoiding the long gradient near Silverton through the Exe Valley.

Driving at snail's pace, the journey home was uneventful until they reached Staunch Hill, on the Tiverton side of Cullompton, near Willand. The van, although loaded with half a ton of equipment and bodies, did not have the necessary traction to surmount the hill. The combined weight of said bodies pushing, and a house brick on the accelerator finally did the trick. The same exercise was successfully carried out near Halberton, on the hill leading to the bridge over the Grand Western canal.

The Falcons were also able to provide a gentleman and his girlfriend, the occupants of a bubble car which was stranded on the hill and could scarcely be seen, with a tow from the brow of the hill. The band, and presumably the cuddling twosome, arrived in Tiverton in the early hours of Sunday morning; the fifteen miles from Exeter having taken in excess of four hours to complete.

It was around this period in 1962 that The Falcons gained a 'cabaret act'. Martin 'Stan' Blythe had moved to Tiverton from Camberley in Surrey where

Say Cheese! (L–R back row) *Brian Nott, 'Smudge' Gratton and 'Bug' Irwin. (L–R sitting) Dave Walker, Martin 'Stan' Blythe and Alan Ferris.*

his parents had run a pub during the war. From a musical family, Martin's violinist mother, Pansy, had constituted one-third of a trio called The Floral Three, the other two members being his aunts, Myrtle and Iris.

Given some steel picks and a steel by his mother, Martin purchased an Hawaiian guitar and learned to play several well-known tunes: 'Midnight', by The Shadows, and the Santo and Johnny classic 'Sleepwalk' being the most popular.

Make yourself at home – Martin Blythe.

Martin's other great love was photography. His father had opened a studio at the top of Bampton Street in Tiverton, naming the business Gainsborough, and had taken publicity photographs of all of the local working bands. Martin assisted his father on many of these assignments, prior to becoming a first-class photographer himself, and was therefore acquainted with all the musicians currently on the circuit, which in turn led to the invitation to join The Falcons.

Martin will perhaps be best remembered, not as a member of The Falcons, but as a superb photographer, many fine examples of which are featured in this book.

The Falcons were undoubtedly a very talented group of musicians, an indisputable fact, proven on many stages throughout the area in august company.

Early in 1963, The Falcons disbanded. 'Bug' Irwin joined his brother in The Strollers; Dave Walker, Alan Ferris and Brian Nott became founder-members of The Starfires, and 'Smudge' Gratton took on the daunting role of vocalist with The Stringbeats.

Martin Blythe, I am delighted to say, decided to pursue a career in photography and lighting.

The Starfires

Many of their fans called them a showband, while others referred to them as rock with brass. The Starfires could certainly lay claim to both titles. Loud and 'in your face', they played with fervour and passion. Exploding, rather than merely arriving on the dance scene, they were an amalgam of musicians drawn from two former Tiverton bands, The Echoes and The Falcons, and from Exeter, The Nightlights. It is debatable whether any Tiverton-based rock group has had such an effect on the dance-going populous in such a short space of time.

The Starfires comprised: lead guitarist Ginger Walker with elder brother Dave on rhythm guitar; bass player Brian Nott; Alan Ferris on drums; and saxophonist Ian 'Fred' Skaines – a veritable feast of musical talent and experience. The compilation of a repertoire, adequate to allow the band to play for a period of four hours or more, was simplicity itself. Ginger would learn the words to a song (most of them anyway), select the key best suited to his voice, and run through the number with his brother. At the next full rehearsal, Brian and Fred would be informed of the song's title and the key in which it was to be played, Alan would work out a drumming pattern, leaving Ginger the elementary task of counting the boys in.

Their first local appearance, on Saturday 2 March 1963, would, for any other band at that time, have been quite daunting. Together with up-and-coming young group The Thunderbirds, they were booked to appear at the Heathcoat Hall in Tiverton, as a support band to national recording star

The Starfires: (L–R) Ian 'Fred' Skaines, Ginger Walker, Dave Walker, Brian Nott and Alan Ferris.

Lance Fortune who, in 1960, had enjoyed chart success with a song called 'Be Mine'.

A telephone call from the singer's office, received by The Starfires' manager Dan'l Wood earlier that week, requested that the boys act as Mr Fortune's backing group on the evening in question and that they make themselves available for a band call (rehearsal), in the afternoon. On their behalf, and with total confidence in the band's ability, the non-musical, but very business-like Dan'l had assured the agent that it would not be a problem.

Lance reached the Heathcoat Hall at lunchtime on the appointed day, having travelled the relatively short distance from Plymouth, where he had given a performance the previous evening. Greeted on his arrival by Dan'l Wood, he was escorted to the stage and introduced to the band. The complete professional, Lance expounded his requirements to the last detail. At five o'clock, with the rehearsal over, a jubilant Lance Fortune was taken to the home of Mr and Mrs Walker Snr for tea.

The evening's entertainment transcended all expectations. Both of the bands played exceptionally well, and the sets performed by Lance 'Be Mine' Fortune, accompanied by The Starfires, gave the enthusiastic audience a night to remember. The dual roles undertaken by The Starfires that evening swiftly brought the band to the attention of dance organisers and agents alike, and they became one of the most popular bands in the South West.

A cancelled booking by a Cornish club-owner, whose refurbishment plans had been unexpectedly advanced, gave the bands a rare, and much appreciated night off, whereupon Ginger announced his intention to go and listen to a band from Exmouth called The Royals who were appearing at the Heathcoat Hall. Together with manager Dan'l and brother Dave, Ginger strolled into the dance hall just as the rather flamboyant manager of The

Guess which one's the singer – The Starfires featuring Kenny Strange.

Royals was issuing a challenge from centre stage, to anyone in the audience who thought they could sing. Goaded by the two Davids, and several fans of The Starfires who were present, Ginger calmly walked on to the stage, gave the band the title of the song he wished to sing and the key in which he wanted it played, duly sang the song and 'brought the house down'.

During the interval which had been called shortly after his 'guest appearance', Ginger was approached by Kenny Strange, the vocalist with The Royals. Kenny had made the assumption that Ginger sang with a band, and asked if there were any vacancies. Living as he did in Plymtree near Cullompton, he continued, it was becoming a chore having to drive the twenty miles to Exmouth for rehearsals. Two weeks later, Kenny became the lead vocalist of The Starfires and, although his stage presence may have at first been a little static, encouraged by the other members of the band, he became a first-class front-man.

Stanley Strange, a butcher by trade and Kenny's father, had recently sold the shop in Cullompton of which he had been the proprietor for a number of years. At the time of his son's defection from The Royals to The Starfires, he had just completed the purchase of a transport café near Whiddon Down, a village close to the A30 between Exeter and Okehampton. A shrewd man, who had always actively supported his son, Stan offered to use his business skills to assist the band in achieving their goal to become a top-flight professional act. Dan'l Wood suggested that Stan take responsibility for the day-to-day management of the band, while he concentrated on stage presentation. Stan's commercial acumen, and Dave Wood's artistic flair ensured that the arrangement worked perfectly, both men being eminently suited to their chosen task.

The Starfires were seldom given the opportunity to play locally. Stan Strange believed that the higher fees were to be found in the larger towns and cities, and the band was placed accordingly. On one occasion, however, they were delighted to find themselves appearing in the parish rooms in Cullompton. The rooms were filled to capacity with appreciative supporters, and the boys' performance was exemplary. At one point during the evening, Stan Strange, from his usual position at the foot of the stage, was somewhat taken aback to hear a girl singing a rock number in perfect unison with his son Kenny. Looking across the room, he was flabbergasted to see the girl jiving at the same time. Ensuring that the young lady was chaperoned, Stan introduced himself, and asked her if she would care to sing a number with the band. The attractive teenager from Cullompton, showing little sign of being nervous, took the stage and sang beautifully. Mary Hasnich, using the stage name Mary Scott, sang with The Starfires for almost twelve months, before joining a band from Taunton called The Sabres. Starfires fans will remember Mary for her duet with Kenny Strange, a cover version of the chart-topping disc, 'Hey Paula'.

'Thank you kind Sir' – Starfires' Mary Hasnich meets actor Ray Brooks.

At the start of 1964, Brian Nott and Alan Ferris left the band; Brian to pursue other interests, Alan to join a band with a less busy workload. Two fine musicians, formerly with The Nightlights, filled their positions; bass player Stuart Boyles, and drummer Terry Denning, both of whom lived in Whipton, Exeter. It took very few rehearsals for Stuart and Terry to become acquainted with The Starfires' playlist, but a little longer to get used to the gruelling five or six nights a week schedule.

After a performance at the Princes Ballroom in Yeovil, Somerset, manager Stan Strange, called the boys together. He told them that, in association with Lionel Digby, head of LMD Entertainment's of Torquay, he had set up a three-date, long weekend in the London area, and that they would leave for the capital on the following Thursday-week.

The big day arrived. The contents of the van were rearranged to allow sleeping bags and blankets to be stowed alongside guitars, amplifiers and drums. A final check to ensure that nothing had been forgotten, and it was off to the bright lights. The journey was uneventful, and the boys reached their destination with ample time to spare. Venue one was a recently opened club called the Rendezvous in Cheshunt, Hertfordshire. The Starfires proved good ambassadors for the West of England, and were well received by an audience of several hundred people.

Day two of the itinerary found Dave, Ginger, Kenny, Fred, Stuart and Terry topping the bill at the massive Streatham Ice Rink. The support act for the evening featured songwriting brothers Ray and Dave Davies, who, with two friends, had formed a band called The Kinks. From the outset, The Starfires played superbly, and they finally left the stage in the early hours of the morning with the applause still ringing in their ears. The Kinks' lead guitarist, Dave Davies, flatly refused to believe that the boys were not professionals, and Kenny got the shock of his life when he was mobbed by dozens of screaming girls anxious to obtain more than just his autograph.

Ray Davies's day had been completely ruined. The Kinks had been totally outplayed by an amateur band from the West Country, and his offer to swap the Gretsch guitar he was currently playing for Ginger's Fender Stratocaster had been politely, but firmly turned down.

The final booking of the tour should have taken The Starfires to the famous 2-Is coffee bar, but sadly it was not to be. Ginger was rushed to a nearby hospital with severe chest pain and breathing difficulties. The diagnosis of the duty doctor was that Ginger was suffering from pleurisy, a condition arising from the inflammation of the tissue surrounding the lungs. Immediate action by the doctor and his medical staff unquestionably saved Ginger's life.

The Starfires returned to Tiverton minus the hospitalised Ginger – and David who had stayed in a guesthouse to be close to his brother – and all bookings were temporarily suspended. After several weeks, Ginger was allowed to return to Tiverton to complete his convalescence in his own home, and Dave began a hasty search for a guitarist to deputise during Ginger's enforced absence.

Sixteen-year-old Barry Sowden, a pupil at the Tiverton Grammar School and lead guitarist of The Avengers, the excellent Geoff Crozier, formerly of The Chekkers and The Staccatos, and a guitarist from the Exeter area called Mike, all helped The Starfires to fulfil their existing bookings until Ginger's return to duty some three months later.

Ginger never regained full fitness and found the rigours of consecutive nights on the road too much. He left The Starfires shortly after elder brother Dave, who, after a difference of opinion with singer Kenny Strange, had ceased to be a member of the band in November 1964.

Classically trained guitarist Stuart Howe from Kentisbeare near Cullompton, and session organist Mike Lloyd, who had recently moved to the area from London, filled the positions left vacant by the Walker brothers' 'retirements', and the band changed its name to The Guild. The outfit was rarely seen on the local circuit, and it was felt by many that The Guild's departure from rock and roll in favour of an almost jazz-orientated style was, perhaps, not for the best.

It should be mentioned that Stuart subsequently won a scholarship to the Guildhall School of Music in London, and graduated in 1970. Mike Lloyd went on to play with Sonny Child, the nephew of legendary Sam Cooke, and his band TNT, and Roy Orbison.

Barry Sowden.

Geoff Crozier.

PHOTO GALLERY

Graham Isaac with Dilendas Vaal.

The Stringbeats: (L–R) Colin Webber, Jo
Phripp, Brian Wright, Mike Herniman.

Nashville Skyline in a roundabout kind of way:
(L & R back) Gerald Orchard and Arthur Ley.
(L & R front) Ray Pope and Barry Sowden.

Johnny and the Strollers: (L–R) Vince Beer, John
Whitter, Colin Roberts, 'Wig' Irwin.

The Cyclones featuring Johnny Carme.

Six 'old bangers': (L–R) John Heady, Ronnie Graham, Ron
Ginger, Bob Jarvis and Ginger Walker.

The Echoes: (L–R) Peter White, Ginger Walker and Paul Midgeley.

The Tuxedos featuring Merv Rainey and 'Bug' Irwin.

Solar System: (L–R) Graham Isaac, Peter Baker, Bernard Swain and Martin 'Benny' Radford.

The Chekkers at Halberton Village Hall, with (foreground) Richard Harder, 'Crockey' Walker and Dennis Moon.

The Southerners: (L–R) John Dray, Brian Nott and Martin 'Stan' Blythe.

57

The Thunderbirds: (L–R) Richard King, Brian Westbrook, Paul Curgenven, Chris 'Kipper' Tree and Tim Tree.

The Falcons featuring Mervyn 'Smudge' Gratton.

POP SPECTACULAR
IN AID OF
The British Empire Campaign for Research
and The Cinema and Television Benevolent Fund
AT ELECTRIC THEATRE, TIVERTON
SUNDAY, 6th JUNE, 1971
at 7 p.m.   Doors open 6.30 p.m.
PRESENTING
The Nashville Skyline
VOCAL HARMONY PLUS THE GOLDEN OLDIES
The WILD HONEY   THE Clothes Peg Family   The BLUE SUNSET
THE WITHLEIGH YOUNG FARMERS   COMEDY SKETCH FROM HYDE PARK
Pete Chowings PRESENTS DISCO '70   SPECIAL GUEST APPEARANCE OF STUART HUTCHISON WESTWARD TELEVISION
Tickets 40p now on sale - Limited Number
DON'T MISS
WOODSTOCK on MON., 7th JUNE & WEEK

After hours with The Ginger Walker Band.

'Crockey', 'Tex' and 'Tub'.

Stringbeats at Dulverton Secondary Modern School.

Johnny and the Strollers at the Heathcoat Hall.

The Echoes at the Heathcoat Hall.

The Cyclones.

Something Different:(L–R) Doug Parish, Mike Herniman and John Bryant.

Shirley and Tony Rawle.

Boing! (Standing, L–R) Gerald Orchard and Ray Pope. (Sitting, L–R) Barry Sowden and Arthur Ley.

(L–R) Jeff Horrell, Jack Cooper, John Dray and Geoff Crozier.

The Groups

PART TWO

The Avengers at Cullompton Secondary Modern School: (L–R) Brian Kingdon, 'Fizz' Saunders, Barry Sowden and Ray Pope.

The Avengers

At the latter end of the 1950s when rock and roll had caught the attention of fun-loving youngsters, and parents were fervently wishing that headphones were more freely available, four young boys from Tiverton decided to form a beat group. The recreation ground in West Exe was a popular meeting place during the summer holidays, and it was there, following a strenuous game of football, and whilst listening to Saturday Club on a small transistor radio, that the decision had been made.

Ray 'Whacker' Sowden.

Ray Pope and Barry Sowden both owned steel-strung acoustic guitars, Morley 'Fizz' Saunders could play a few tunes on his tenor saxophone, and Ray 'Whacker' Sowden volunteered to play drums. He put forward the argument that, although Barry owned the snare drum, stand and sticks, he could not play the guitar and drums at the same time, so as a member of the family, it was only right that he, Whacker, help out.

Practice sessions, to the relief of the Sowden and Saunders families, were held at the home of Ray's parents in John Street. Barry would play the melody, with Ray strumming accompanying chords. Fizz, with annoyingly apparent ease, would play what the boys would later learn to be a counter melody, and Whacker would fully live up to his nickname. In retrospect it is hard to believe that Michael took such a long time to row the flaming boat ashore, ten rehearsals at least, but hallelujah!, this and a couple of dozen other songs were sufficient to convince the lads that the effort was worthwhile. A vocalist however was urgently needed. Whacker learned that his friend Peter Hammacott had won a talent contest at Butlins while on holiday, and invited him to join the group as its singer. The months flew by and the season of goodwill to all mankind arrived. Ray and Barry posted requests to Father Christmas and were rewarded on the morning of 25 December with a Framus electric acoustic, and a Broadway Guyatone solid guitar respectively. On Boxing Day afternoon, Mr Pope Snr gravely informed his son and his friend Barry, that the elderly lady across the road had suggested that they practise elsewhere.

L–R: *Morley 'Fizz' Saunders, Barry Sowden and Ray Pope.*

Peter Hammacott.

A storeroom above the fruit and vegetable shop in West Exe North owned by Fizz's father became the band's new 'home'. Also new, a Watkins Westminster amplifier, a microphone for Peter and an electric Hofner President bass guitar for Fizz, who had decided to change instruments, all provided by Peter's father, Maurice Hammacott, who was to be repaid by the boys with their wages from two paper rounds, a bread round and two 'willing shop assistants'. Three electric guitars and one microphone plugged into a 15 watt amplifier, which in turn, was connected to the mains via a bayonet light fitting; that the amplifier, guitars and mike buzzed a bit but

Robin Hayball.

Dave Walker.

actually worked, and that the premises never caught fire, was really quite incredible.

Instrumentals were the orders of the day and, on the pretext of hero worship, chords and approximate finger positioning were cribbed from local guitarists Pete White, Paul Midgeley, Ginger Walker, and his brother Dave, among others, at their rehearsals (thanks guys!).

A love for the game of soccer, to the exclusion of all else, caused Peter and Ray Sowden to leave the band after six months or so. Brian D. Kingdon an apprentice hairdresser, joined the group as its drummer, and Ray Pope startled everyone by announcing that he would take over the vocals, on the grounds that he knew the lyrics to a couple of Buddy Holly songs. Ray did in fact know the words of all Buddy Holly's songs, and possessed a fine voice with which to sing them.

After months of rehearsing, and with more than a little help from guitarists Rob Hayball and Dave Walker, the boys felt that they were competent, and confident enough, to perform with an audience. When asked to play in the War Memorial Hall, Tiverton for the members of the Royal British Legion, they proudly did so with only minor hiccups, such as the tailpiece of Barry's top of the range Broadway Guyatone guitar (costing £12), falling off. Work commitments, and GCE examinations respectively, saw Brian and Fizz leave the band, but replacements were swiftly recruited, in the form of Geoff Bulley on drums, and Brian 'Cockbird' – for such was his nickname – Knowles on bass guitar.

With the changes in personnel, came the need for additional rehearsal. Ray, Barry, Geoff and Brian, all being nightly visitors to the comparatively new, purpose-built, youth centre at Bolham Road, made representation to the long-serving, popular, and highly-respected leader Leonard 'Curly' Harder, asking for the use of a large room on the first floor. The request was granted on the condition that the band take part in a variety show being organised by centre members, in aid of local charities. The amateur production, stage-managed by assistant leaders Frank and Ray Berry, was held in the main hall at the secondary modern school, and was a huge success. Without doubt, the Egyptian sand dance, performed by Geoff Smyth and Brian Knowles, and the spoof ballet, again featuring Geoff Smyth, but partnered on this occasion by 'dainty' Dan'l Wood, were the highlights of the evening, but the entire cast acquitted themselves well.

It was just prior to the aforementioned show that The Avengers gained a female singer. Janet Berry, pretty daughter of Frank and Ray, was at one of the Sunday afternoon rehearsals in the youth centre, practising a song for the forthcoming event. Geoff Bulley, having listened to Janet's rendition of 'You Made Me Love You', rounded up Ray, Barry and Brian who were in the committee room on the first floor drinking coffee, and informed them that there was a girl downstairs with a terrific voice. Having played at the centre the previous evening The Avengers' gear was still set up and Janet was asked if she would like to use the band's PA system, and perhaps let the boys back her. Hearing an affirmative reply Barry swiftly sorted out the chords and Janet sang her first song as The Avengers' leading lady. Equally at home belting out rock numbers or ballads, she was with the band for about twelve months.

Frank and Ray Berry.

On 13 March 1965 The Avengers took part in an audition for the television programme Opportunity Knocks. Held at the Festival Theatre in Paignton in the presence of Hughie Green and Miss Monica Rose, they exceeded their expectations by taking second place, Janet almost winning the heat for the band with her version of the Pony-Tails' hit 'Born Too Late'. To complete a busy day, she and the boys were the supporting act for Screaming Lord Sutch and the Savages at the Queen's Hall, Barnstaple, in the evening. Before her departure in 1966 to pursue a career in medicine as a radiographer, Jan continued to front the band, which by this time had become extremely popular. In addition to headlining their own gigs The Avengers supported many of the top acts performing at the Tiverton Youth Centre: The Applejacks, The Four Pennies, Peter Jay and the Jaywalkers, ex-Searcher Tony Jackson and his band The Vibrations, and The Bystanders to name but a few.

Janet Berry.

In the early part of 1966, The Avengers were 'summoned' to a meeting at the youth centre by Derek 'Dodger' Green, their manager who stated that, in his opinion, drummer Geoff Bulley was uncooperative and should be replaced. Ray, Barry and Brian, vehemently disagreeing with both statements, insisted that not only would Geoff stay with the band, but that they would dispense with the services of a manager.

Now responsible for their own destiny and free from any managerial encumbrance, the boys decided to implement a number of changes. The Avengers at Geoff's suggestion became The Order, and began looking to albums for their material rather than the Top Ten, a trait that was continued by Nashville Skyline in years to come.

TIVERTON
YOUTH CENTRE
PRESENTS
THE
FOUR PENNIES
SUPPORTED BY
TIVERTONS
OWN
AVENGERS
FRIDAY NOV 5th 1965
8 00 pm. til MIDNIGHT
Admission 5/-

Agents and, more importantly, the loyal following built up by The Avengers

In 'playful' mood at Tiverton Youth Centre: (L–R) Barry Sowden, Brian Knowles, Geoff Bulley and Ray Pope.

The Order.

appeared to like the 'new band', continually demonstrating their approval by attending dances whenever and wherever The Order were on the bill.

Booked at Seaton Town Hall as the support act to chart-topping Billy J. Kramer and the Dakotas, The Order were into only their second number when Barry broke a string on his guitar and sheepishly announced that he had forgotten to buy a spare set. Suffice to say that the other three members of the band were not best pleased! Apologising to the 300 or so people present, Barry dived backstage and 'borrowed' a string from the Dakotas' lead guitarist Robin. Quickly fitting and tuning the scavenged string, Barry returned to the stage and the band completed the evening with no further problems.

At the post-performance inquest, emotions were mixed. Ray was angry, Brian was livid, and Geoff was positively fuming! He had seen Barry earlier in the day, and reminded him to get a set of spare strings. Barry's excuses fell upon deaf ears, and he was warned that should the same thing happen again, he would be thrown out of the band. Barry's reply hardly reflected his grammar school education, 'If that's your attitude, you can shove it!'

The Order employed guitarists Tim Tree and John Banwell as a stopgap for about a year following Barry's departure, but when Brian Knowles left Tiverton to join the RAF, Ray and Geoff agreed to call it a day and The Order was wound up in 1967.

The Dominoes

Born in 1941 to a farming family at Clayhanger, a small village on the Devon and Somerset border, Tony Rawle would watch spellbound as his mother carefully unlocked and began to play the piano which stood in the front room of the farm house. Fascinated by the sound emanating from the instrument, his love of music started at a very tender age.

Persistent requests to be allowed to play the piano fell upon 'deaf ears', but when he reached the age of eleven his parents relented, and enlisted the aid of a piano teacher. The strict practice regime was not to Tony's liking and the tutor's visits were discontinued after only six lessons. The lessons had, however, provided him with sufficient rudimentary skills to demonstrate to his disappointed parents his determination to master the instrument, albeit at his own pace.

During the next two years he played the piano whenever possible, and could play most of the melodies popular at the time, both from the music and 'by ear'. Seeking a new challenge he asked to be given a piano accordion for his thirteenth birthday. On this occasion his parents were more than happy to accede to his request having had visual and aural proof of their son's musical aptitude.

The accordion's portable nature allowed Tony to practise his craft even more regularly, and once again his abiding faith in his own ability was proven. He gained confidence with each day that passed and, when asked to entertain the members of the local Women's Institute at their forthcoming meeting, did so with a confidence that belied his years. This inaugural public performance gave vent to a flurry of invitations to play at functions in other villages around the area. It was at one such event in the village of Ashbrittle, that Tony met Louis Woodman.

Drummer Louis Woodman who, with pianist Frank Hannaford, played regularly at the Half Moon public house in Clayhidon, had been impressed by the teenager's performance, and asked him if he would like to join them on Saturday nights. Tony's acceptance of the offer effectively changed the 'singalong style' pub duo into a more modern, pop-orientated dance trio.

Although the evenings spent with Frank and Louis provided Tony with invaluable experience, there were many occasions when he was double-booked. Local commitments eventually persuaded him to found his own band with Louis Woodman and a young lad, also from Clayhanger, Roderick Milne. Tony thought he had the potential to become a very good guitarist and backed his judgement by purchasing an electric guitar and amplifier for

The Dominoes at Shillingford Village Hall: (L–R) Rod Milne, Gerald Orchard, Shirley Rawle and Tony Rawle.

him. He was reimbursed by fourteen-year-old Rod in weekly instalments, from monies earned with the equipment. A microphone was mounted on the top of his accordion, allowing Tony to simultaneously sing and play in a sitting or upright position, dispensing with the need for a boom-type microphone stand; then the trio were ready to start rehearsing.

Their first rehearsal was a memorable occasion. Firstly, because it was decided to call the band The Dominoes, and secondly, because Tony's left arm was heavily bandaged due to an accident on the farm. In the months that followed, it became evident that Tony was accident-prone, prompting Rod to enquire whether he could actually play the accordion without his hands or arms bandaged or in plaster!

With very little advertising, news of the band's formation quickly spread, attracting enquiries and requests for its services from Young Farmers', cricket and football clubs.

After a busy evening at Shillingford Village Hall, Tony's customary ten-minute unwinding session was interrupted by a boy named Gerald Orchard. Complimenting Tony on his performance Gerald mentioned that he too was a farmer's son, and that he could play the guitar. Thanking him for his comments, Tony invited the boy to bring his guitar to the band's next rehearsal.

Gerald Orchard.

An apprehensive Gerald duly reported to Fleeds Farm, the ancestral home of the Rawle family, where he familiarised himself with enough of the band's repertoire for Tony to suggest that he deputise for Rod if the need ever arose. Sound in wind and limb, Rod gave him precious few opportunities to play his guitar as a fully-fledged member of The Dominoes, but Gerald was ever-present during rehearsals, and an ardent supporter of the band at dances.

He finally became a member of The Dominoes in 1966, when Louis Woodman was tragically killed in a road traffic accident near Tiverton.

Gerald had played Louis's drum kit on a number of occasions, usually after rehearsal, or when the dance hall had emptied, and in truth, was a far better drummer than guitarist. Gerald's purchase of a Premier drum kit coincided with Tony's decision to forsake the accordion in favour of a single manual Hammond organ. The tonal qualities of the Hammond gave The Dominoes a distinctive sound, which was instantly recognisable.

Shirley, Gerald and Tony.

On 1 April 1967 Tony married Shirley, a girl he had met at Skilgate Village Hall some two years previous. By the autumn of the same year her husband had persuaded Shirley, a charming girl with a pleasant singing voice, to sing four or five songs in each half of a Dominoes' performance. As her anxiety abated and her confidence swelled, Shirley's personal repertoire increased, and she became an integral part of the band.

In the summer of 1968 Rod left the band to concentrate on his A-level examinations. The Dominoes were playing on three or four, and occasionally five nights a week, a schedule leaving little time for revision. Not wishing to leave the music scene completely, Rod joined a band called Cloud 49 with, from Willand near Cullompton, organist Frank Harris and drummer Phil Spearing, and from Cullompton, bass player Dave Retter.

Playing perhaps once or twice a month, Cloud 49 was probably best termed a hobby band. It was a very loud hobby band, a fact to which the reporter, sent by the *Tiverton Gazette* to listen to them playing at the East Devon College in Bolham Road, Tiverton, will surely attest. In the 'Teenage Grapevine' column of the following week's issue of the newspaper, the cub reporter stated that the band could be clearly heard in Park Road, more than half a mile away.

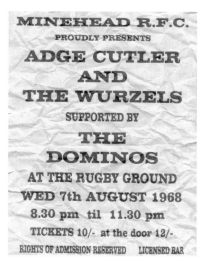

MINEHEAD R.F.C.
PROUDLY PRESENTS
ADGE CUTLER
AND
THE WURZELS
SUPPORTED BY
THE
DOMINOS
AT THE RUGBY GROUND
WED 7th AUGUST 1968
8.30 pm til 11.30 pm
TICKETS 10/- at the door 12/-
RIGHTS OF ADMISSION RESERVED   LICENSED BAR

Rod's departure from The Dominoes caused Tony Rawle to suggest that he teach his wife to play the bass guitar. On 27 July 1968, a mere six weeks later, Shirley and her Hofner violin bass, as used by Beatle Paul McCartney, lined up with husband Tony and drummer Gerald Orchard at Lynton Town Hall for her debut performance. It proved to be an eventful evening. Drained of energy, having helped the boys haul the equipment up three flights of stairs to the ballroom, and extremely fretful, Shirley timidly but faultlessly played her way through the first number. After an hour or so, she began to really enjoy herself, the odd mistake appeared to go unnoticed and the applause seemed genuine. When Tony announced that the band would be taking a short break, she was surprised to learn that they had been playing for over two hours. On her way to the bar for a well-earned drink, Shirley was 'horrified' to meet guitar ace Brian Wright. Already self-conscious, and now in the presence of one of the best guitarists in the South West, Shirley wanted to go home. One of the very nicest of people, and aware of the fact that she was nervous, softly- spoken Brian had nothing but praise for Shirley's playing, assuring her that she was doing fine, and that the band sounded good.

The intake of two or three glasses of liquid from a bottle labelled Smirnoff, and Brian's cheery wave as he and his friends left the hall, reunited Shirley

I can play that!

and her confidence. Her playing was basic but accurate, and she sailed through the rest of the evening.

At the start of 1969, in constant pursuit of excellence, Tony proposed that a lead guitarist be recruited, and that the name of the band be changed. Gerald suggested that he contact Ginger Walker who, he thought, might be available. At an informal meeting following Ginger's acceptance, no one could think of a suitable name for the 'new' band, and the subject remained pending.

The secretary of a local football club, and a friend of many years, asked Tony to place an advertisement in the much-read and highly respected *Tiverton Gazette*, for a forthcoming dance at which the, as yet unnamed, band were to appear. Tony obligingly furnished the young lady at the office in Tiverton with the details of the venue, the date, and the price of tickets etc. Asked to give the name of the band Tony replied, 'Oh, I don't know; just put a question mark'.

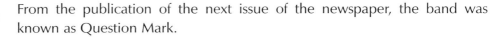

From the publication of the next issue of the newspaper, the band was known as Question Mark.

Ginger Walker.

The addition of Ginger Walker to the line-up gave Question Mark the option of playing traditional, or modern dance music, which widened an already substantial support base. Question Mark's supporters were loyal, and apparently impervious to anything, or anyone attempting to spoil their enjoyment. This was proven at Exford Village Hall when a 'gentleman' who had consumed considerably more than the recommended daily amount of alcohol, thought it a good idea to discharge a fire extinguisher in close proximity to the band. The fellow was ejected from the dance and the police notified. Question Mark resumed their performance, and it was business as usual.

Ginger Walker left Question Mark in July 1971 and was replaced by former member Rod Milne. In December 1971, Question Mark disbanded.

Tony and Shirley Rawle intended to start a family, and Gerald had been invited to join Nashville Skyline. Rod decided to commit himself to a business enterprise with which he was involved, but would never become completely divorced from the music scene.

Question Mark's final appearance at a filled-to-capacity Shillingford Village Hall was a very emotional one. Tony recalls that they played well past the time that the event was to have finished, and the ovation following the last number was such, that it will always remain a cherished memory.

How much!

If, in the context of a pop trivia quiz the question was asked, 'Who are the Gibb brothers?' the reply would inevitably be 'Barry, Robin and Maurice', or alternatively 'The Bee Gees'. Knowing folk from Pennymoor would answer 'Brian and Desmond from Furze Farm.'

At the age of ten, Brian, the elder of the two brothers was given a button accordion, which, under the watchful eye of his piano-playing mother, he learned to play reasonably well. Doug Parish, living at Cruwys Morchard and a friend of the Gibbs, would join Brian and Desmond on Sunday afternoons with his Hofner Spanish guitar and the three boys would, as Doug put it, 'Kick up a rattle' in the garage, everything being played in the key of G, with Des hitting oil drums, milk churns and the like in the absence of a drum kit.

With the advent of The Shadows came Brian's decision to abandon the 'squeezebox' and buy a guitar. Unfortunately, his fingers were not sufficiently long enough to hold down basic chord shapes, and the dream of showing Hank Marvin a thing or two went the same way as the button accordion. Not to be beaten, however, Brian initiated plan B. Having occasionally banged away at mum's piano when she was out of the house and successfully obtaining the odd recognisable tune, he resolved to learn to play the instrument properly. Three years of hard work in both theory and practice followed, and an enviable level of competence resulted. On 14 June 1965 Brian completed the purchase of a Farfisa compact organ priced £165 from Bill Greenhalgh in Exeter. At rehearsals the following day, Brian discovered that the organ had a minor malfunction. One of the keys produced a note that

The Shakey Notes at Clapps Café, Tiverton: (L–R) Desmond Gibbs, Doug Parish and Brian Gibbs.

seemed to quiver, an effect known to musicians as tremolo, causing Desmond to remark, 'That note's a bit shaky Brian!' Almost undetectable during a rock number, and skilfully avoided when playing a ballad, the troublesome key went unrepaired, but it did provide the band with a name, using the American spelling because it looked better when written.

Prayers to St Cecilia, the patron saint of music, and equally fervent entreaties to mums and dads were answered when Desmond collected his first drum kit, and Doug Parish took possession of a Guild Starfire electric guitar and Selmer amplifier. The boys were now 'ready to rock!'

In October 1965 The Shakey Notes played in public for the first time, at Cruwys Morchard Village Hall, using on this one occasion bass player Peter Guscott. The boys' faces were wreathed in smiles when they were given £1 each at the end of the evening.

The New Year arrived, and brought with it a booking from the local Young Farmers' Club to play at their belated Christmas party. This was the turning point for the trio, and an exceptional performance on the night put them firmly in the minds of many visiting club secretaries, to the extent that by 1967 the boys were playing at least twice a week, and had invested in new equipment and stagewear.

Vocalist Arthur Ley had often sat in with Brian and Des when the brothers were performing as a duo at the Cadeleigh Arms, and officially became a member of The Shakey Notes in 1968. Arthur left the band, now called The Shakey Notes Plus in July 1969 to join Nashville Skyline, a defection copied by Doug Parish shortly after. Guitarist Peter White and Singer Mervyn 'Smudge' Gratton were brought in to replace the Skyline-bound Arthur and Doug; but the band never really recovered from their departure and The Shakey Notes Plus disbanded in March 1970. Barely two months later Brian, Desmond, Peter and Doug Parish, who had recently parted company with Nashville Skyline, were back on the circuit as Blue Sunset, Doug now playing bass guitar and singing lead vocals.

There was to be one more significant change in the line-up. Fine young guitarist Graham Isaac, formerly with hard-rock outfits Zyeuter Haze and Solar System, was added at the expense of rhythm guitarist Peter, who freely admitted his shortcomings in the lead guitar department. Graham's presence and playing style had an almost immediate effect on the band which, from playing easy listening, middle-of-the-road numbers, turned to hard hitting covers from the charts. After a three-year period during which they appeared at venues throughout the length and breadth of Devon and Somerset, the boys by general assent, and feeling the need to pursue other avenues within the business, took the decision to disband, the final gig being at the Honiton Motel on New Year's Eve, 1972.

Lead guitarist Graham Isaac joined Exeter-based Dilendas Vaal who were signed with BCD Entertainments of Bodmin in Cornwall, and in

Three Plus One: (L–R) Tony Bale, Brian Gibbs, Rosalyn Truelove and Tony Truelove.

consequence spent a lot of time working in that particular area of the country. Doug Parish strayed from the live music path with Johnny Ramone's Atlantis Discotheque, but was soon to be back on stage as vocalist and bass player with the band Something Different. Drummer Des Gibb returned to within half a dozen miles of his Pennymoor roots by teaming up with father and son John and Dave Chapple from Witheridge, as a conventional dance trio called The Red Stars.

Bandleader and organist Brian, after a twelve-month sabbatical, formed Three Plus One, a 'middle-of-the-road' band with guitarist Tony Truelove and his sister Rosalyn. Experienced drummer Tony Bale completed the line-up. At the end of 1974, Tony was recruited by country band Denver Spur to play pedal steel guitar, his place in Three Plus One being taken by vocalist and guitarist Charlie Page from Hemyock.

Playing mainly in North Devon and Somerset through the auspices of well-known Chard agent Frank Huddy, the band became quite popular – but clashes of personality, and what Brian describes as constant hassle, became all too common, and in November 1975 he and Charlie decided to leave Three Plus One.

Founding their own band with the provisional name Freewheeler, the long-standing alliance with Frank Huddy's Double H agency as Three Plus One was renewed, and this, coupled with local demand, kept Freewheeler in the public eye. A long-playing vinyl album entitled 'Alright on the Night', financed and marketed by Mr Huddy, was well received by the band's supporters.

Albeit with an ever-changing combination of musicians, Freewheeler were to continue in the musical arena for many years, the ever dependable Brian Gibb remaining the one constant throughout.

Nashville Skyline

The year was 1969, and Tiverton Barbell Club had a problem. In an effort to raise badly needed funds, they proposed to hold a dance. The venue, Clapps Café in Gold Street, Tiverton, had been booked, and the sale of tickets and door stewarding arranged. Unfortunately, there were no bands available on the date required.

A telephone call from club member Kenny Foxford to Geoff Bulley, saw Ray Pope, Barry Sowden and Geoff once again take the stage, Ray switching from rhythm to bass guitar in the absence of Brian Knowles who had left the area. The band rocked their way through the evening, playing many of the numbers which had made them so popular in their heyday as The Avengers and The Order.

The occasion was supposed to have been a one-off, but some three weeks later, Doug Parish and Arthur Ley, who had just left The Shakey Notes Plus, linked with Ray, Barry and Geoff to form a new band with the provisional name of Aquarius. Ray, however, did not like the name and suggested Nashville Skyline, a title he had 'lifted' from one of Bob Dylan's albums. The rest, as they say, is history.

The Order at the New Hall, Tiverton.

A single rehearsal held in the village hall at Sampford Peverell enabled Doug and Arthur to learn many of the numbers previously played by The Order. The additional harmonies provided by the former 'Shakeys' gave Nashville Skyline an enviable vocal flexibility which was to prove popular with promoters, agents and dance-goers alike.

The first real test for the new band came just a fortnight after its formation. Nashville Skyline was asked to appear at the New Hall, Tiverton, on Friday 12 September as the support act for a band called Cupid's Inspiration, a professional outfit from Lincolnshire, who had recently enjoyed huge success with a song entitled 'Yesterday Has Gone'.

Skyline's lively, and polished performance on the night in the presence of such august company, prompted Terry Rice-Milton, the highly talented lead vocalist with Cupid's Inspiration, to suggest that they turn professional and take their sound on the road. Serious consideration was given to Terry's comments, but family ties and regular employment won the day.

Nashville Skyline were perhaps lucky in that bands like The Starfires and The Strollers were part of Tiverton's musical history, and even more fortunate because The Variations were out of the equation. It was nonetheless gratifying that Skyline became, quite simply, the band everyone wanted to book.

Down in the jungle something stirs! (L–R) *Gerald Orchard, Arthur Ley, Barry Sowden and Ray Pope.*

It was a tribute to the band's rising popularity, when they were asked to accompany singer Johnny Ramone on a permanent basis. This merging of talent brought incursions on to the cabaret circuit, and the band found themselves performing in some of the South West's finest hotels and clubs. Dress suits and bow ties were in, the comfortable shirts and jeans gone, but certainly not forgotten, as Skyline loved to play in and around Tiverton whenever their seemingly perpetual workload allowed, and could relax in front of a home crowd. It became the norm to have just two, or perhaps three, nights off each month, the rest being spent at Warren Beach Holiday Camp, Sladnor Park Country Club in Torquay, Exmouth Pavilion, Devon Valley Holiday Centre at Shaldon and Hookhills at Paignton, amongst others.

PRIVATE PROMOTIONS PRESENT

VALENTINE'S BEATNITE

WITH

THE ALAN BOWN

AND

THE NASHVILLE SKYLINE

THE NEW HALL, TIVERTON

FRIDAY, 13th FEBRUARY, 1970

8.30 p.m. to 1 a.m.

Rights of Admission Reserved   No Admission without Tickets after 10.20 p.m.

No Admission or Re-admission after 11 p.m.

TICKETS 12/-   AT THE DOOR 14/-   LICENSED BAR

It has been said that Johnny Ramone's voice was perhaps a little too sweet for rock and roll, but it cannot be denied that he was the area's premier singer of ballads and a fine club entertainer. The combination of Johnny's cabaret act and the self-contained routines of Nashville Skyline married extremely well, but was largely responsible for a minor exodus.

Doug Parish and Arthur Ley had been lead vocalists with their previous band, relishing their position as front men. With Ray Pope handling Skyline's lead vocals, and the infusion of John's cabaret sets, Doug and Arthur felt that they were contributing little more than backing. For this reason Doug left Nashville Skyline in February 1972. He became the lead singer and bass player with Pete White's new band Touch of Amber early in 1973, and was soon reunited with drummer Geoff Bulley when he too joined Touch of Amber. Arthur remained a member of Nashville Skyline until becoming the final piece of the Touch of Amber jigsaw in March 1973.

Nashville Skyline: (clockwise from top left) Ray Pope, Rod Allcock, Johnny Ramone and Gerald Orchard.

Nashville Skyline's first priority was to recruit a drummer. Auditions were held at Clapps Café over the space of two evenings, and there were eight applicants for the vacancy. Once again, lady luck smiled on the two surviving members of Skyline. A much travelled and experienced drummer, Gerald Orchard, was among the applicants. Gerald's timing and expressive style was ideally suited to the type of material being played by Ray and Barry. A ten-minute run-through, three or four numbers at most, and Gerald was offered the position. Thus, with a minimum of rehearsal, Nashville Skyline plunged headlong into six hectic years, during which they played to audiences across the county in both summer and winter seasons.

Ultimately, of course, the pressure of this demanding workload took its toll. Nerves became frayed, disagreements were commonplace and tempers often flared. Blows were never exchanged, but it was a very close thing on many occasions. Barry was the first to 'crack'. He left the band, his place being taken by a fine guitarist who had recently moved into the area from the North of England, Rod Allcock. After nine months or so, in a second bout of lunacy, Barry accepted an invitation to rejoin Skyline.

The group disbanded on 29 July 1979 after completing a performance at Willey's Social Club, Exeter. The three musicians were in agreement not to use the name Nashville Skyline for any bands that they may form in the future, unless at least two of the three were members of that band.

Since that day, there have been several Skyline reunion gigs to aid numerous charitable organisations, and the boys remain good friends. Ray formed his own band, Time and Again, with Rod Allcock on lead guitar and drummer Chris Bowden. Barry joined a country band from North Devon and Gerald became a very much in demand freelance, prior to joining Freshwater.

In final analysis, some twenty-three years later, Nashville Skyline is still fondly remembered and often copied, but never quite matched.

Time and Again: (L–R) Ray Pope, Chris Bowden and Rod Allcock.

The Hotspots

The divide between old-time dance music and rock and roll was neatly bridged by The Hotspots. The group was formed in the early 1960s by former Bluebirds' accordionist John Bryant and guitarist Fred Davey who, like John, lived in Witheridge. Drummer Jeff Stevens from Copplestone near Crediton, and electric and Hawaiian guitarist Dennis Knight completed the founding quartet.

Shortly after its debut performance at the Cadeleigh Arms public house, the quartet became a quintet with the addition of saxophonist Terry Cottrell who had been 'poached' from The Bluebirds. Additionally, Bernard Rew was ever willing to swell both the ranks, and the overall sound, with either clarinet or saxophone.

The presupposition that the 'swinging sixties' would sound the death knell for traditional dance bands like The Hotspots could not have been more wrong. As has already been well documented, dance promoters were extremely reluctant to turn from the melodic, tried and tested music, and beat groups were experiencing great difficulty in obtaining bookings.

The original Hotspots.

The Hotspots at Wallingbrooke Hall, Chulmleigh.

Like The Bluebirds, The Hotspots were very busy, playing on both Friday and Saturday nights to packed halls in and around the Tiverton and Crediton areas. When Fred Davey left the band to visit pastures new, an advertisement was placed in the 'Situations Vacant' columns of the *Melody Maker* magazine announcing the fact that The Hotspots required a guitarist. Several guitarists purporting to be capable and adaptable answered the advertisement, but few were willing to relocate to the West Country.

Not the Dave Clarke Five: (L–R) Keith Gowan, Terry Cottrell, John Bryant, Paul Hutchings and Mike O'Connor.

Living up to his apt surname, guitarist John Westward left his home at Leytonstone, North London, and moved to Witheridge. Lodging and working with John Bryant at C.P. Unwin Ltd, he played with The Hotspots for a number of years before returning to the capital.

By 1964, The Hotspots had cultivated a large following, and it was not unusual to see the same faces at dances on consecutive evenings, even if the two venues were many miles apart. One loyal supporter, an Irishman called Michael O'Connor, would invariably present himself at the foot of the stage and ask if he could sing a couple of songs. This became such a regular occurrence that he was eventually invited to join the band. Also recruited during the consolidation period were bass player Paul Hutchings and vastly experienced drummer Tony Harper who had replaced Jeff Stevens. The line-up then remained virtually unchanged until the end of the decade, the one exception being Keith Gowan who had taken over the drumming duties from Tony Harper – the man who had taught him to play.

Paul Hutchings and Mike O'Connor parted company with the band at the latter end of 1969 – Paul for personal reasons and Mike, it is understood, returned to Ireland.

The Hotspots were doubly fortunate in that Ginger Walker had recently been made 'redundant' by the demise of Question Mark and was not presently

Live at the Narracott Grand Hotel in Woolacombe, North Devon: (L–R) Terry Cottrell, John Bryant, Keith Gowan, Ginger Walker and Bob Jarvis.

working with any other outfit, and bassist Bob Jarvis, a relative of Bluebirds' accordionist Cyril Blackford, was available on a free transfer from an Exeter-based combo called The Red Aces.

The complete entertainer Ginger Walker and the accomplished Bob Jarvis breathed new life into The Hotspots. The ability to play old-time and modern music with equal aplomb had mass appeal. A favourite 'party piece' was to perform the Top Ten songs in the current Hit Parade (the Charts), followed by a waltz or a quickstep. This versatility brought engagements throughout the county, and to perform on five evenings each week was quite normal.

The band also made frequent incursions into the North Cornwall district and these visits were rarely incident-free. Booked to appear at Bridgerule on behalf of the Young Farmers' Club, the boys met with time to spare in the car park of the Thelbridge Arms public house, near Witheridge, owned by the parents of drummer Keith Gowan. The equipment was transshipped from private cars into Keith's 15cwt Ford Thames van; the drive to the venue was unremarkable and the hall in which the function was to be held easily found.

Keith's van prior to the Jarvis modifications.

The anticipation of an enjoyable night was displaced by the realisation that a brown shopping bag containing mains, speaker and guitar leads had been left behind. With two hours remaining prior to the commencement of the fes-tivities, Bob Jarvis volunteered to return to Thelbridge and collect it. In sight of the Thelbridge Arms and the completion of the first leg of his journey, Bob failed to negotiate a tricky bend at Bill Hole Quarry and generally restyled the van's bodywork, simultaneously rendering the radiator useless.

Shaken, and only slightly stirred, Bob pushed the van around the corner into the pub car park, jumped into his own van – a Bedford Dormobile, which incidently, contained a brown bag full of leads identical to the one which had been forgotten, and drove safely back to Bridgerule. The evening proved to be a rip-roaring affair and the boys were tired but happy as they loaded the equipment and themselves into the little Dormobile and started for home.

Bob was the recipient of some good-humoured banter. John Bryant stated his intention of writing a book extolling the virtues of advanced driving tests, and Ginger enquired if Bob had passed his driving test in a tank during the war. With assumed disdain, Bob let the mockery pass as he carefully manoeuvred the vehicle up the narrow country lane leading to the A3072 Holsworthy–Crediton road. Spotting a sharp bend ahead, Bob suitably adjusted his speed and approached the corner. Bob recalls, 'I turned the steering wheel and nothing happened.' The van ploughed into the hedge throwing the musicians and the equipment forward.

Terry Cottrell ran to the main road and flagged down a passing motorist, who conveyed the band to Stratton hospital where their various injuries were treated, and garage proprietor Kit James was summoned from Witheridge to recover the Dormobile.

The following evening, still in shock and badly bruised, The Hotspots played to a full house in Burrington, North Devon. Keith Gowan remembers that he played 'sort of one-handed', but nobody noticed any difference!

In 1973 the band went into the studios of Solent Records and cut an extended-play vinyl disc entitled 'What's New', which featured four original songs: 'Can't Understand', 'Spend My life', 'For What You got', and 'I'm a loser – I'm a loser', all of which were penned by Ginger Walker.

This was also the year in which saxophonist Anton Kaiser joined the band. Born in Germany, Anton was employed by John Heathcoat & Company, and was introduced to Ginger Walker. Anton was a member of The Hotspots for almost two years before returning to Germany.

On Friday 9 February 1974, The Hotspots were booked to appear at The Barnstaple Hotel. On the same day at about 1pm, Ginger's pregnant wife Sue experienced her first contraction. Ginger contacted his colleagues in the band and informed them that he wished to be at the birth, but that he would get to the gig as soon as Sue had had the baby.

Sue had their baby at midnight, and Ginger failed to arrive at Barnstaple. So did John Bryant. John had made the assumption, that without Ginger the date would be postponed. The band were able to complete the engagement, however, thanks to a young keyboard player from Barnstaple called Jonathan Brown, the son of the area secretary of the Musicians' Union, and known to bass player Bob Jarvis.

Early the next day, Ginger received a telegram from the lady owner of the Narracott Grand Hotel in Woolacombe, stating that she had heard that he was not at the Barnstaple Hotel the previous evening and that The Hotspots had split up. The telegram went on to say, 'The Hotspots are due to play at the Narracott tonight, please confirm!' Ginger went immediately to a call box, rang the hotel and reassured the owner on both points. On their arrival that evening, the boys were given a bottle of champagne in celebration of Ginger's new baby and that The Hotspots were still very much a going concern.

Some weeks later Keith Gowan fulfilled a dream when he emigrated to Australia. At the same time, John Bryant reluctantly accepted that he could no longer cope with the punishing seven-nights-a-week schedules, and briefly retired from the scene.

Vocalist and keyboard player Brian Westbrook, who had often guested with The Hotspots, and drummer Geoff Bulley joined Ginger, Bob and Terry in forming a 'new band'. It was agreed that the name Hotspots should be updated in deference to the more modern outlook of the band, and the title of The Solent recording 'What's New', was tentatively adopted. The Coast to Coast Bandwagon later superseded this identity.

The Bandwagon became a showband, featuring comedy, impressions, four-part vocal harmony, fancy dress, bingo and the throwing of 'custard pies'; their popularity steadily increased. Although all five musicians had attended the semi-professional academy and graduated in the subject of 'the effect on the human body of late nights and early mornings', the strain of performing each night of the week in addition to holding down 'a proper job' was beginning to tell.

The option to turn professional was one that merited consideration and details of the outcome can be found in the biography of The Ginger Walker Band that follows later in this book.

Newly booted and suited: (L–R): Terry Cottrell, Brian Westbrook, Ginger Walker, Geoff Bulle and Bob Jarvis.

Something Different

It is very difficult for the majority of musicians to get off the semi-professional treadmill that has been part of their life for many years – and virtually impossible to stay off it. So it was with John Bryant and Doug Parish. Meeting quite by chance in the bar of the Stag Inn at Rackenford, the conversation between the two musicians went something like this:

John: 'Alright Doug?'
Doug: 'Hello Mate, How's tricks?'
John: 'Bored stiff – you still doing discos?'
Doug: 'Nah – got cheesed off!'
John: 'Yeah – know what you mean.'
Doug: 'Heard you left The Hotspots.'
John: 'Yeah – they were playin' five, six and sometimes seven nights a week – 'twas too much!'
Doug: 'Yeah – I don't think I could hack that.'
John: 'D'you fancy doing the odd gig?'
Doug: 'What – Just us two?'
John: 'Nah – We'll get a drummer – I think Herniman's spare.'
Doug: 'Good drummer! – d'you fancy another beer?'
John: 'Thought you'd never ask – I'll have a pint ta.'
Doug: 'What're we gonna call this band then?'
John: 'Oh I don't know – something different.'
Doug: 'Good enough!'

Fortunately, drummer Mike Herniman was available and joined John and Doug in founding the area's latest band – Something Different.

Mind where you're putting that drumstick! (L–R) *John Bryant, Doug Parish and Mike Herniman.*

The practice sessions – held in the function room at the Stag Inn – were largely unnecessary. The three musicians possessed a wealth of experience gathered over many years – John with The Bluebirds and The Hotspots, Dougie with The Shakey Notes and Mike with The Stringbeats and The Variations. A playlist – sufficient to 'carry the band' through a four-hour stint – was compiled in the course of one evening.

News of the band's formation spread. Locally at first, the trio began to receive requests for their services. Each completed engagement served to act as an advertisement for the band and they were very soon venturing further afield.

Surprisingly, Something Different appeared to be more popular in the North Devon area, although the band was highly rated by many social clubs within the city of Exeter.

The secretary of a social club in Taunton, Somerset, referred to Something Different as 'a proper party band'. He continued by saying, 'They turn up on time, they're tidy, and there's nowt they won't have a bash at!'

The versatility and modest volume of the little trio was reassuring to social clubs with elderly members, and/or smaller premises, although the boys were always prepared to 'give it some', when the opportunity presented itself. From 1972, the year of the band's formation, until 1977, when the three musicians amicably parted company, Something Different succeeded where many rock outfits failed, by playing the sort of music that the fee-paying general public wanted to hear, and not what the band wanted to play.

Doug Parish and Mike Herniman were later to reunite as members of a band called Bender, with former Stringbeats' rhythm guitarist Rick Gray.

John Bryant went into semi-retirement from the music business, but was regularly asked to play in his immediate locality, and accepted many such invitations gladly, teaming up on these occasions with old friends Digger Ford or Frank Creegan. Frank, from Templeton near Tiverton, possessed a fine singing voice, and the combination of his crooning style and John's experienced playing was a popular addition to any pub's entertainment.

Two's Company: John Bryant and Frank Creegan.

Something Different at St Thomas's Cricket Club.

Touch of Amber

Take one bespectacled rhythm guitarist with an encyclopaedic knowledge of chord shapes (of which there are thousands), add one bass guitarist with a penchant for singing rock and roll, blend gently with a voice that could easily double for Barry Gibb of The Bee Gees, and beat thoroughly with the best rock drummer Tiverton has ever produced. Place in a hot dance hall for about four hours and the result is a Touch of Amber.

Founded in 1973 by guitarist Peter White, with Doug Parish, Arthur Ley and Geoff Bulley, Touch of Amber was an immediate success. Within weeks of its formation, the band was assigned to play the South Devon circuit in tandem with Nashville Skyline. Surprisingly, the band in this format did not stay together long. Doug Parish left and formed Something Different with organist John Bryant, and Geoff Bulley became a member of Ginger Walker's latest 'kit-form' outfit, his place being taken by John Lucas from Bow, near Crediton.

Over the next few months, Peter, Arthur, John and a host of stand-in bass players struggled to produce a performance level that met with individual approval. This, coupled with an element of unreliability within the band, was sufficient cause for Peter to make wholesale changes.

Long-time friend and former 'Echo' Paul Midgeley, vocalist David Wright (stage name Johnny Royal), and the ex-bass player with Ginger Walker, Malcolm James, were recruited and with existing members John Lucas and Peter completely transformed both the sound and the type of material played, with an instrumental set being a highly popular and integral part of the band's repertoire.

'Neath the spreading chestnut tree: (L–R) Malcolm James, Jeff Kitson, Paul Midgeley, Brian Westbrook and Pete White.

With the exception of drummer John Lucas, who due to business interests left the band shortly after this renaissance, being replaced by a youthful Jeff Kitson, the new Touch of Amber played into the middle 70s, gaining respect throughout Devon and Somerset.

1977 brought not only the Silver Jubilee, but more changes to what had been a relatively stable Amber line-up. The departure of Johnny Royal and Jeff Kitson for reasons unknown, heralded the arrival of much-travelled vocalist and keyboards man, Brian Westbrook, and drummer Chris Bowden. Lead guitarist Paul was, for the second time in his career, admitted to hospital to undergo surgery on a troublesome back. Although the operation was considered a success, Paul's playing days were sadly over and it is a moot point as to whether this was the beginning of the end for Touch of Amber.

In the years that followed, Peter White tried numerous permutations of musical talent in an effort to retain, and possibly enhance, the reputation that had been built. Former members Arthur Ley, John Lucas and Malcolm James, saxophonist Terry Cottrell, bassists John McCulloch and Chris Barnard, the husband and wife team of Barry and Jean Hyatt on guitar and keyboards respectively, and drummer Kevin Sussex, all figured in what were to be the final days of Touch of Amber.

EXMOUTH & DISTRICT ROUND TABLE

HOLLY BALL

AT THE EXMOUTH PAVILION

ON FRIDAY 8th. DECEMBER 1978

The Ginger Walker Band and Touch of Amber

8.30 p.m. — 2 a.m.   Dress: Lounge Suits

TICKETS £1.50

The Ginger Walker Band

In 1953 there were no discotheques, no nightclubs and the pubs closed at 10pm. 'Nimrod's Nectar' Scotch whisky cost 4s.6d. a bottle, and it was possible to obtain a modern gas cooker from the South Western Gas Board on hire purchase terms for one shilling (5p) per week (fixed and maintained free). More relevantly, it was the year in which Ginger Walker started playing the guitar. Twenty-four years later, he took the biggest gamble of his life by leaving the employ of John Heathcoat & Company to become a professional musician.

The Maurice Price Orchestra: (L–R) Vic Palmer, Tony Osborne, Maurice Price, Colin Drake, Don Brooks, Ron Ginger and Ray Hill.

The Ginger Walker Band: (behind, L–R) Ginger Walker and Ronnie Graham. (In front, L–R) Ron Ginger and Bob Jarvis.

The Hotspots had often discussed the merits of taking the professionals' route. The band was hugely popular and the boys had unanimously agreed to limit their performances to a mere five evenings per week. Business interests, family constraints and regular employment were among the reasons sufficient to persuade Brian Westbrook, Terry Cottrell and Geoff Bulley to retain their semi-professional status. Bass player Bob Jarvis, however, rose to the challenge and, like Ginger, turned professional.

Band leader Vic Palmer was probably not best pleased when his superb drummer Ronnie Graham left to join Ginger's band, but the balance was restored when Geoff Bulley made the trip in the opposite direction.

A saxophonist, whose surname would suggest that he could have got a job with the new band regardless of his musical prowess, provided the final piece in the meccano set that was The Ginger Walker Band. Equally competent on both clarinet and flute, Ron Ginger completed the line-up.

Is this a record?

Keeping to the tried and tested principle of playing what the people wanted to hear, the band quickly became established. Rehearsal was rarely necessary, it was simply a matter of, 'Here's the key, just follow me.' The boys were normally preceded by their reputation, and were soon working with many of the big names from the swinging sixties: Gerry and The Pacemakers, The Hollies, Marmalade, The Fortunes and The Searchers and from the world of jazz, Chris Barber and Kenny Ball, amongst others.

I COULDN'T BELIEVE MY EARS !!

In 1978 the band recorded a long-playing album entitled 'I Couldn't Believe My Ears'. On selective release, many hundreds of copies were sold. The next year saw the production, again on selective release, of two singles, the first being a song called 'Dulciana Clarabella', and the second, a double A-side disc: on side one, 'Panda Cars', which featured pupils from Heathcoat Primary School in Tiverton, and on the flip side, the old Billy Cotton standard 'Friends and Neighbours', which allied Ginger's voice to those of the Exeter

The GINGER WALKER Band

Police Choir. Incidental 'vocals' by Barry and Mary Sowden and Ray and Maureen Pope were added to the latter of the two discs and used during the fade-out sequence.

At the end of 1978, Ginger was pleased to inform his band that they had no free dates available during the forthcoming year. In addition to a seven-month summer season in North Devon, the band was to play in virtually every major city in the land.

Whilst the full diary gave the band both stability and financial security, Ginger was fully aware that any request to book the band during 1979 would have to be turned away, and with this in mind he resolved to start an Entertainment's Agency.

Ginger Walker Entertainment's Agency has, since its founding in 1979, become a name synonymous with quality and service, and a highly successful enterprise. Long may it prosper.

Ginger Walker with Exeter Sound Recordings boss John Greenslade and children from Heathcoat Primary School.

The New Bluebirds and Barracuda

At the age of fifteen, Fred Harris was indentured as an apprentice motor mechanic to Derek 'Digger' Ford, proprietor of the Hare and Hounds Garage in Witheridge, and drummer with The Bluebirds dance band. In these early days, Fred was more than happy in the knowledge that a working day would contain not only instruction in the complexities of the internal combustion engine, but tales of village hall dances, and the extraordinary lengths to which his employer and fellow band members would go to ensure that all instruments arrived at a venue in reasonable, if not mint condition.

In 1968 Fred bought his first guitar, and with the aid of Bert Wheedon's 'Play in a Day' tutor (an extremely optimistic boast in the majority of cases), learned to strum a few chords, eventually joining The Bluebirds – the other members of which were accordionists Cyril Blackford and Peter Boax, and drummer Digger Ford – as rhythm guitarist and vocalist, performing for the first time with the band at Molland Village Hall.

Shortly after Fred's acceptance of full membership, Cyril Blackford decided to become a part-time player allowing him to devote more time to his farm.

(L–R): *Martin 'Benny' Radford, Derek 'Digger' Ford and Cyril Blackford.*

His place was taken by accordionist Martin 'Benny' Radford, soon to be the son-in-law of Peter Boax.

The new-look Bluebirds were equally, if not more popular, than the original, and although the rock outfits in Tiverton were now established, the little dance band continued to be in demand. After many years, Digger Ford was forced to accept the fact that he could not combine the management of a garage, his duties as a retained fireman, and his much loved hobby – that of drumming with The Bluebirds. Digger reluctantly handed the 'engine room' of the band into the capable hands of drummer and accomplished keyboard player Frank Bond – a friend of Benny's from the Technical College in Tiverton.

Prior to joining The Bluebirds, Fred Harris had occasionally entertained the Withleigh Young Farmers' Club, and it was at one of these evenings that he met bass player, Ivor 'Snacker' Nott. A left-hander, Ivor, from the hamlet of Worlington, subsequently taught Benny to play the bass guitar, his adopted instrument in later years.

By the middle 70s, the boys were regularly requested to play rock and roll at dances held throughout the area and Fred, Benny and Frank were happy to

The New Bluebirds: (L–R) *Martin 'Benny' Radford, Frank Bond and Fred Harris.*

oblige. Peter Boax, certainly one of the most accomplished piano-accordionists in the district, cared little for this type of music and clearly stated his opinion on the subject. Peter eventually came to appreciate that the band would have to play rock and roll to obtain bookings, but stuck to his principles and let the boys get on with it.

For about twelve months the band played under the banner of The New Bluebirds, but decided to change their identity in line with the more modern music they were playing, and at the start of 1978 The New Bluebirds became Barracuda.

A polished and blended mixture of old-time, country and rock music made Barracuda an extremely marketable commodity, and their fan base stretched from coast to coast.

On 16 July 1983, a day Fred describes as one of the worst of his life, Benny died in a tragic accident at work. Promoters were contacted and all bookings cancelled. Many months passed before Fred and Frank were able to face the prospect of playing again. Eventually, however, John McCulloch was recruited as bass guitarist and Barracuda were back on the circuit.

Doug Parish later replaced John McCulloch, and the line-up of Fred on rhythm guitar, Doug on bass and Frank doubling on keyboard and drums, remained unchanged for the next eight years.

Frank Bond died in 1998, but will be remembered as a very talented musician, with a wonderful sense of humour.

For a number of reasons, Doug Parish left the band at the end of 1991, and Fred, as Ray Pope had done many years before, made the transition from rhythm to bass guitar. Fred, ironically, still uses a Fender bass once owned by Ray. Guitarist Mike Barkworth became a member of Barracuda in January 1992, and he and Fred are much in demand as a duo, but can often find themselves fronting three- or four-piece versions of the band, tailored to the

Barracuda plus: (L–R) Tony Ruby, Mike Barkworth, Fred Harris, Gerald Orchard and Frank Bond.

promoter's requirements, by using drummers Gerald Orchard or Mike Herniman, and saxophonist Tony Ruby.

Barracuda recently celebrated twenty-five years in the music business with an invitation evening at Tiverton Town Football Club, the proceeds from which were donated to the local hospital.

The twenty-five years' span (1954–1979) encompassed by this book was extended to the present day for Barracuda because, unlike any other band featured, they are still very much in existence and continue to delight audiences wherever and whenever they take the stage.

♩ ♫ ♪

A Band of Absent Friends

Derek 'Digger' Ford – drummer – The Bluebirds.

Stan 'Bungy' Beer – double bass player – The Bluebirds.

Peter Boax – accordionist – The Bluebirds.

Frank Bond – keyboard player and drummer – The New Bluebirds and Barracuda.

Martin 'Benny' Radford – accordionist and bass player – The Bluebirds, The New Bluebirds and Barracuda.

John Vanstone – vocalist – The Cyclones.

Brian Wright – lead guitarist – The Vampires, The Stringbeats, The Variations, The Academy and Freshwater.

Bob Grabham – drummer – The Echoes.

Stuart Boyles – bass guitarist – The Starfires.

Ray Pope – rhythm and bass guitarist – The Avengers, Nashville Skyline and Time and Again.

Louis Woodman – drummer – The Dominoes.

Paul Hutchings – bass guitarist – The Hotspots.

Tony Harper – drummer – The Hotspots.

Ronnie Graham – drummer – Vic Palmer Combo and The Ginger Walker Band.

William 'Bill' Greenhalgh – violinist and saxophonist.